Bay Area Bike Rides

RAY HOSLER

Chronicle Books • San Francisco

Printed in the United States of America.

Library of Congress Cataloging-in-Publication Data

Hosler, Ray.
   Bay area bike rides / Ray Hosler.
      p.   cm.
   Includes index.
   ISBN 0-87701-568-6
      1. Bicycle touring—California—San Francisco Bay Area—Guide
-books.   2. San Francisco Bay Area (Calif.)—Description and travel
—Guide-books.   I. Title.
GV1045.5.C22S264   1990   89-35341
917.94′6—dc20   CIP

Editing: Julie Pechilis
Book design: Seventeenth Street Studios
Cover design: Julie Noyes
Photography: Ray Hosler

10   9   8   7   6   5   4   3   2

Chronicle Books
275 Fifth Street
San Francisco, California 94103

Bay Area Bike Rides

Contents

Acknowledgments, vii
Introduction, ix
Bicycles on Public Transit, xiii
Bay Area Ride Locator, xv
Key to Maps, xvi

II. OFF-ROAD RIDES

III. CASUAL RIDES

Acknowledgments

A heartfelt thanks goes to the following individuals who helped me research, edit, and write *Bay Area Bike Rides:* Jobst Brandt for leading the way on rides and giving editorial advice; Michael Kelly for leading rides in the East Bay; Jim Westby, Ted Mock, and others for riding along; Joe Breeze for the Mt. Tamalpais mountain bike ride; William Ziegler for printing the photos; and all of the government agencies and libraries that provided invaluable information.

Introduction

With quiet country roads to ride against scenic
backdrops, Northern California fulfills the dream
of every bicyclist. Add to this the seemingly endless variety of available routes, and you have some
of the best bicycling anywhere in the world. After
a decade of bicycling over the hills and through the
valleys of San Mateo and Santa Clara counties, I
still find each ride a new adventure. Even in light
of the phenomenal growth we've seen in the Bay
Area, bicycling can be a carefree and car-free experience if you know where to go.

Most rides in *Bay Area Bike Rides* are within an
hour's drive for Bay Area residents. Many can be
reached by public transportation, such as Bay Area
Rapid Transit (BART), ferry lines, or county bus
service; your bicycling possibilities can thus be
expanded without involving a lot of driving.
Mountains, flatlands, cities, or rural parks —
they're all easily accessible.

Here's one example of how you might combine
bicycling with public transit and park touring:
Take the ferry from San Francisco to Sausalito,
bicycle to Muir Woods National Monument, lock
your bike, and tour the majestic old-growth redwoods on foot. You can ride home over the inspir-
ing Golden Gate Bridge or return via the ferry.

What's more, in the Bay Area bicycling is a
year-round activity. It's hard to say which season is
best for bicycling because every month has its
appeal. In the spring I like to ride over Mt. Hamilton to see the wildflowers. In the summer there's

nothing more invigorating than a cool ride on the foggy Pacific Coast. In the fall the remote reaches of the Santa Cruz Mountains display autumn colors and have the refreshing smell of decaying leaves following the first rains. In the winter I often ride to the bay for birdwatching or visit local parks to hike.

Your bicycling pleasure will be enhanced if you're well prepared. Weather changes by the hour and by the mile, especially between bay and ocean and between low and high elevations. Dress appropriately. Be prepared for encounters with cars and other obstacles. Always be alert and never assume motorists know what you're doing. Although car encounters are few and far between for most cyclists, remember you're not the only person using the road. Ride single-file on narrow roads. You're almost always better off avoiding confrontations with motorists: Unless you're looking for trouble, ignore rude or inattentive drivers.

Be aware that roads which I've identified for touring may have been changed, rerouted, torn up, repaved, or even shut down since this book went to press. It can't hurt to check with a local bicycle shop about road conditions if you're traveling some distance to a ride.

Even more uncertain is the status of off-road riding. Be sure to check with a park ranger who can tell you which trails are open to bicycles. Mixed trail use has become a major issue in our increasingly popular urban—and even rural—parks. Mountain bikers have begun to use trails previously frequented only by hikers, and unless they prove that they can ride safely and responsibly, bicycles will be banned from these trails. This has already happened in some Bay Area parks. Bicycles are permitted on narrow hiking trails in only a few locations in the Bay Area. The "trails" described in the off-road rides are mostly old logging or service roads ideal for all trail users. Ride no faster than 15 mph and pass other trail users at reduced speed, usually 5 mph or less. But most importantly, have control of your bicycle at all times and be able to stop quickly.

The book is divided into three sections: Road, Off-Road and Casual. Road rides are completely on pavement. Off-road rides take place on dirt, although you'll also be riding on pavement on many occasions. Casual rides are located in parks and recreation areas where you'll stay on recreation paths away from traffic. Use caution passing pedestrians and don't go over 10 mph.

Usually it's best to do casual rides early in the morning to beat the crowds. The best time for road rides is early weekend mornings when traffic is light. If you start by 8 a.m. you'll avoid traffic, the air will be fresh and cool, and you'll finish your ride at a reasonable hour. Most stores open on Sunday by 9 a.m., in time for a food break.

I've included some local history to give you a sense of how much life has changed in the Bay Area over the past 25 years. Think how it must have been a century ago when this fertile land was sparsely populated. Most of the roads you'll ride on were built between 1850 and 1890 for logging and railroads. And the courses chosen by the original road builders were sometimes along foot paths used by the Costanoan Indians. Other roads were built for special purposes, like that up Mt. Hamilton, which was constructed for access to the summit's telescope observatory. Parts of Highway 9 and Highway 236 were built in the early 1900s to connect Big Basin State Park with Santa Clara Valley and Santa Cruz.

You will notice that many of the rides involve some climbing. Most can be accomplished by riders of all ages and abilities who have the proper gearing and conditioning. In time you will realize that enjoyable riding, whether it be for scenery or to avoid traffic, is easy to find in the hills. If you're new to bicycling, you may want to start with casual rides and gradually increase your distance. Casual rides take place on flat terrain. When choosing a road ride, carefully study the terrain profile on the map to get a better understanding of what to expect. Give yourself plenty of time to complete the ride, and don't forget to bring food or money to buy a snack. Most of the routes pass at least one store or shopping center where you can get a bite to eat.

I wrote this book to include something for everyone. The longest ride is 104 miles, the shortest less than four miles. There are hilly, mountainous, and flat rides. Every ride was measured using an Avocet bicycle cyclometer, with all turns, rest stops, and points of interest noted in the Mileage Log. A bicycle computer will reduce your chances of getting lost. Please note that mileages involving a turn or important intersections are shown in bold face. Enough said. Let's go for a bike ride.

Bicycles on Public Transit

Bicycles may be transported on BART, ferries, some buses, and light rail in the San Francisco Bay Area. Some restrictions apply and may change without notice, so check with the agencies before using them.

BART. Bike permit required. Travel restrictions during commute hours (you can travel in reverse commute directions on some lines during commute hours), but none on weekends, holidays and noncommute hours. A three-year permit costs $3. For a free three-week temporary permit ask at any primary station. For a five-page "Bikes on BART" brochure that describes the procedure and rules, and to purchase a permit, write to BART, 800 Madison St., P.O. Box 12688, Oakland, CA 94604-2688. Phone (415) 464-7133 or 464-7135.

Santa Clara County Transit. Bicycles are permitted on all bus lines in Santa Clara County, but only when there is room available and at the discretion of the driver. A rack for two bikes is attached to the front of the Route 300 bus, which runs weekdays between Palo Alto and San Jose on El Camino Real; first-come, first-served. You must be at least 16 or accompanied by an adult 21 years or older. Operators cannot leave the bus to assist you. For more information: County Transit, Bikes on Route 300, P.O. Box 4009, Milpitas, CA 95035-2009. Attn: Commute Alternatives. Phone (408) 287-4210.

San Jose Light Rail. Extending from Santa Clara to San Jose, the light rail allows no more than two bicycles on the last car at the rear only. Phone (408) 287-4210.

Caltrain. Providing daily service between San Jose and San Francisco, Caltrain allows folding bicycles only, and they must be contained in a bag. For information write to Caltrain, Dept. of Transportation, Rail Management Branch, P.O. Box 7310, San Francisco, CA 94120.

Bay Ferry Service. All of the San Francisco Bay ferries servicing Sausalito, Larkspur, Tiburon, and Vallejo permit bicycles for free. Golden Gate Transit operates between the San Francisco Ferry Building and Sausalito and Larkspur seven days a week. The Larkspur ferry provides commute service only during weekdays. For information call (415) 453-2100, (415) 546-2896, or (800) 445-8800. The Red and White Ferry operates Monday through Friday between Sausalito and Tiburon and San Francisco's Ferry Building. Angel Island and Tiburon are serviced daily during the summer, and on weekends and holidays during the winter. For information call (415) 546-2815.

AC Transit (Alameda and Contra Costa Transit Authority). The "T" line bus crossing the San Francisco–Oakland Bay Bridge between San Francisco, Oakland and Alameda will carry up to four bicycles. It runs seven days a week, every half hour during the commute, otherwise hourly. There is also a Bay Bridge Bicycle Commuter Shuttle weekdays only. A 12-passenger van tows a trailer holding 12 bikes. Fee is $1. For information about the T line call (415) 839-2882; for Commuter Shuttle call (415) 464-0876.

Sam Trans. San Mateo County buses permit bicyles, but only if the tires are removed and the chain is covered, and then only at the driver's discretion.

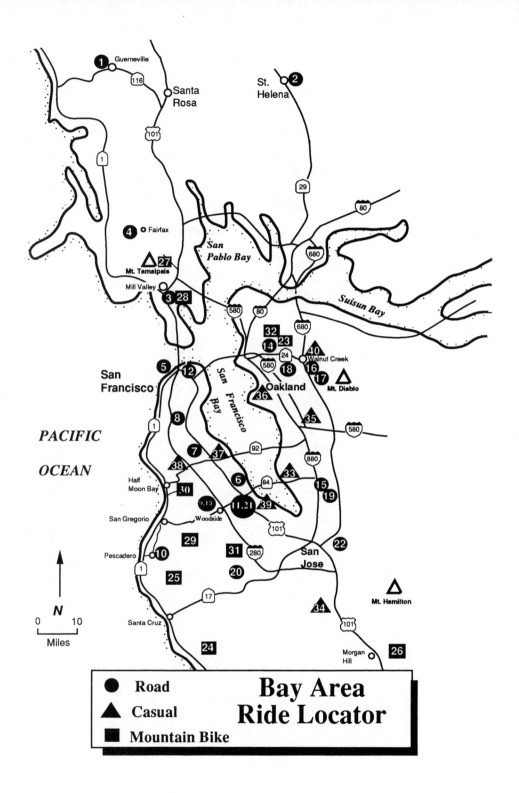

Guerneville
①
116
○ Santa Rosa
101
1

St. Helena
②

29

80

④ ○ Fairfax

San Pablo Bay

△ 27
Mt. Tamalpais

Mill Valley ○
3 28

680

Suisun Bay

580 80 680

32
14 23
△ 40
24 Walnut Creek
580 18 16
17 △
Mt. Diablo

⑤ 12

San Francisco

San Francisco Bay

36 Oakland

35 △

580

PACIFIC

⑧

OCEAN

1

⑦ 37
92
880
38
Half Moon Bay
30 ⑥ 84 33
9,13 15
Woodside 11,21 39 19

San Gregorio

29
101
22

Pescadero
⑩ 31 280
San Jose
25 20

1

17
34 △
Mt. Hamilton
Santa Cruz
101

N
0 10
Miles

24

Morgan Hill ○ 26

● Road
▲ Casual
■ Mountain Bike

Bay Area Ride Locator

Key to Maps

Paved road (major)		Interstate	280
(minor)		U.S. Highway	101
Dirt road or trail		State Highway	1
Paved path		Airport	
Route		American Youth Hostel	
Parking (Ride Start)	P	Ferry	
Parking (Other)	P	Fort	
Creek		Gate	
Old growth redwoods or unique tree		Golf course	
Town or city	O	Heliport	
Altitude or point of interest	●	Lighthouse	
Mountain top	△	Oil Well	
Campground			
Observatory		Radar dish	
Park headquarters or building		Windmill	
Railroad tracks		School	

I. Road Rides

1. Russian River Valley

Distance: **61 miles.**
Terrain: **Hilly.**
Traffic: **Light to moderate.**

If you ride on Sonoma County backroads to the Pacific Coast you'll discover acres and acres of redwoods, a pristine and rocky Pacific shoreline, and sheep grazing on grassy meadows.

A good place to start your ride is the rustic town of Guerneville on the Russian River. The town was founded in 1865 near a sawmill that supplied railroad ties for the transcontinental railroad. In its early years it was called Stumptown for the many tree stumps left by loggers who cleared the land. Later the town was renamed Guerneville after George Guerne, an early mill owner.

Spring and fall are the best seasons for riding here, although it can be pleasant in the winter and invitingly cool along the coast on hot summer days. Temperature differences of 20 degrees between the coast and the river valley are common in the summer. Winds start gusting at mid-morning and generally blow from the north along the coast.

Park on Main Street (Highway 116) downtown and bike out of town heading west on Highway 116. This two-lane road is most heavily used in the summer when vacationers come to enjoy the river. Old Cazadero Road is on your right in a half-mile, but continue straight. Old Cazadero turns to dirt and requires fording Austin Creek before reaching the town of Cazadero.

Turn right on Austin Creek Road 6.6 miles into the ride. This old, narrow road to Cazadero is lightly traveled. Tracks of the narrow-gauge North Pacific Coast Railroad ran along Austin Creek at

Mileage Log

0.0 Start mileage in downtown Guerneville at intersection of Highway 116 and Mill Street. Ride west toward the ocean on Highway 116.

0.6 Old Cazadero Road. Do not turn here. Road goes through to Cazadero but requires fording Austin Creek and has lots of climbing.

6.6 **Right on Austin Creek Road.**

10.1 **Left onto bridge over Austin Creek.**

10.2 **Right on Cazadero Highway.**

12.9 Town of Cazadero. Restrooms at tennis courts often closed. Has one main store open every day.

▼

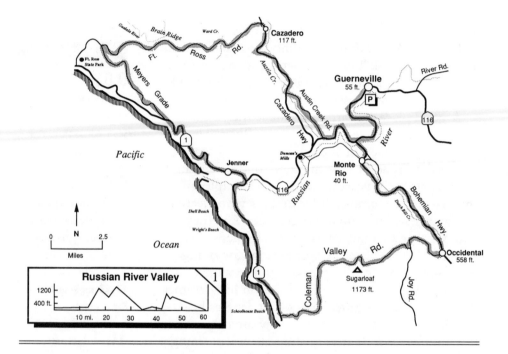

Russian River Valley

13.3 Left at junction with King Ridge Road onto Fort Ross Road. Begin steep climb.

18.5 Summit. Begin 2.3-mile descent and level section.

▼

the turn of the century and were traveled by trains hauling logs to Duncan's Mills on the Russian River and passengers to Sausalito.

You'll follow Austin Creek Road for several miles before crossing a bridge to pick up Cazadero Highway, a wide, smooth road that follows the equally wide and shallow Austin Creek. At 12.9 miles you'll reach Cazadero, formerly a bustling logging town, nestled in a canyon. Today it's a quiet village, with two churches, a public tennis court, a few stores, and the Cazadero Inn.

Cazadero Highway becomes Fort Ross Road on

the way out of town. Keep left at the Kings Ridge Road junction; this portion of the route was once included in the Coors Classic bicycle race. The complexion of the ride changes as the road climbs steeply from 177 feet to more than 1,400 feet. The first of the two major climbs that bring you to this elevation is the steepest. Turn back now if you're not up for a lot of climbing.

Fort Ross Road winds through wild and scenic rolling hills among the redwoods and Douglas fir, although you'll notice the toll that forest fires have taken in recent years. One attraction that characterizes this region is the rough-hewn redwood fences, bleached gray by the weather and decorated by lichens in various shades of green.

After a roller coaster ride on Fort Ross Road turn left on Meyers Grade. On a day without coastal fog you can see the Pacific from amidst green meadows, redwoods, and conifers.

The rugged coast and surf become visible as you begin a breathtaking descent to Highway 1. Watch for sheep on the road and for cattle guards, which deserve caution, especially when wet.

On Highway 1 you will pass Sonoma Coast State Beach with its many areas of public access. Watch for seals packed together like driftwood at the mouth of the Russian River. The village of Jenner makes a good food stop. There's an interpretive center with a small pier and restrooms at the bottom of the hill.

Continue south on Highway 1 for nine miles to Coleman Valley Road, where you'll turn left and climb a steep hill for less than a mile to an exposed ridge with numerous rock outcroppings. A row of cypress lining the road marks the turnoff. In the spring you'll find iris along the road and sheep in the meadows. Traffic is light on the narrow, bumpy road except on warm Sundays in the spring.

In the wooded Coleman Valley there's an old ranch with a few barns. From the valley you'll have a short climb and then a descent to the town of

22.4 Left on **Meyers Grade at stop sign. Summit.**

25.5 Begin descent to Highway 1.

27.3 Left on Highway 1 at stop sign.

31.7 Town of Jenner. Restrooms and food at mile 32.5. Restrooms next to Russian River at interpretive center.

33.6 Right at junction with Highway 116. Cross Russian River.

40.2 Left on Coleman Valley Road. Watch for row of tall cypress.

41.7 Top of steep part of climb. Gradual ascent to mile 45.5.

46.5 Coleman Valley.

48.1 Begin climb out of valley. Summit at mile 48.8. Begin 1.5-mile descent.

50.3 Left at stop sign in town of Occidental onto Bohemian Highway. Road becomes Main Street a half-mile from Monte Rio.

▼

These newly eroded islets on Highway 1 south of Meyers Grade are known as sea stacks.

56.7 **Town of Monte Rio. Left at stop sign onto bridge over Russian River.**

56.9 **Right at junction. Begin Highway 116 after stop sign.**

60.9 End of ride in Guerneville.

■

Occidental, best known for its Italian restaurants and bed and breakfast inns.

Complete the loop by returning on Bohemian Highway, a long gradual downhill through the redwoods along Dutch Bill Creek. Ride through Monte Rio, cross the Russian River on a narrow bridge (there's a sidewalk you can ride on), and then turn right to return to Guerneville on Highway 116.

2. Napa Valley

Distance: **16 or 54 miles.**
Terrain: **Flat on short ride;
hilly on long ride.**
Traffic: **Light to heavy.**

Napa Valley is a collage of colors all year, but most of all in the fall when grapevines display greens, reds, and yellows. Fall is also one of the best seasons to visit this world-renowned wine region. The grape harvest is over, the summer crowds have left, and cool mornings give way to delightfully warm days. On weekends you can see colorful hot-air balloons and gliders riding updrafts near the rocky red cliffs of The Palisades near the town of Calistoga.

St. Helena, an unpretentious town in the center of the valley (population 5,000) between Napa and Calistoga, is suited for both bicycling and wine tasting. In years past local residents have enjoyed watching the Coors Classic bike race, one of many valley events with an international flavor. Past courses have gone over Oakville Grade and along Silverado Trail.

Both the short and long ride listed in the Mileage Log begin in St. Helena. The short ride loops through the valley, passing more than 20 wineries, including Sutter Home, Louis Martini, Robert Mondavi, Christian Brothers, and other famous names.

Start early to avoid traffic on Highway 29. Most wineries are open from 10 a.m. to 4 p.m. for tasting. Silverado Trail is a two-lane road with a wide shoulder, the best route through Napa Valley for safe cycling. Train tracks crossing Highway 29 at two locations are a hazard to bicycles because they cross the road diagonally. You may want to dismount to cross safely.

Mileage Log

Ride #1
Valley Tour

0.0 Park at St. Helena High School south of intersection. Start mileage at intersection of Pope Street and Highway 29. Ride east on Pope Street.

0.8 **Right on Silverado Trail at stop sign after crossing stone bridge over Napa River.**

5.3 ZD winery on right.

7.3 **Right on Oakville Cross Road.**

9.8 **Right on Highway 29 at stop sign.**

11.8 BV winery on right. Beware of train tracks on Highway 29.

▼

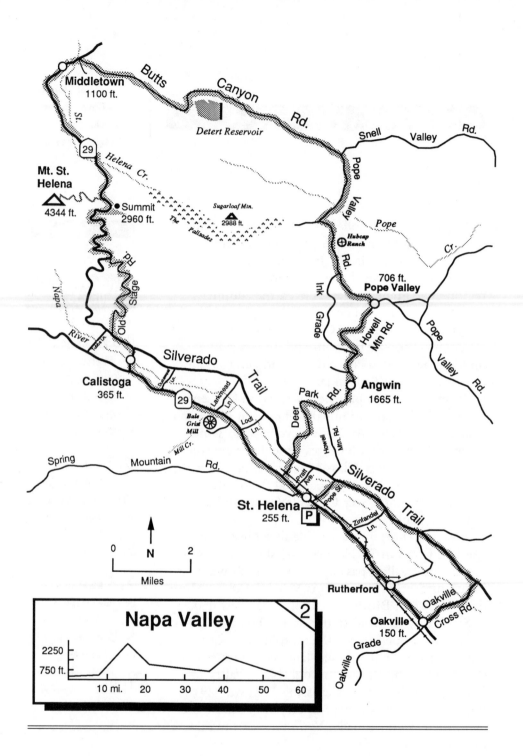

Middletown
1100 ft.

Butts Canyon Rd.

Detert Reservoir

Snell Valley Rd.

Mt. St. Helena
4344 ft.

Summit
2960 ft.

Sugarloaf Mtn.
2988 ft.

The Palisades

Pope Valley Rd.

Pope Cr.

Hubcap Ranch

706 ft.
Pope Valley

Napa River

Old Stage Rd.

Silverado Trail

Ink Grade

Howell Mtn Rd.

Pope Valley Rd.

Calistoga
365 ft.

Bale Grist Mill

Larkmead Ln.

Lodi Ln.

Deer Park Rd.

Angwin
1665 ft.

Howell Mtn. Rd.

Spring Mountain Rd.

Mill Cr.

St. Helena
255 ft.
P

Pratt Ave.

Pope St.

Zinfandel Ln.

Silverado Trail

0   N   2

Miles

Rutherford

Oakville Cross Rd.

Oakville
150 ft.

Oakville Grade

Napa Valley

2

2250
750 ft.

10 mi.   20   30   40   50   60

On the long ride you can stop and visit the Bale Grist Mill, which has a giant wooden waterwheel 36 feet in diameter, weighs 5.5 tons and could generate 40 horsepower. It was built in 1846 by Dr. Edward Bale. The flour mill closed in 1905; in 1974 the mill became a state historic park and restoration began in 1980; one day the giant wheel will turn again.

Cyclists seeking scenic rewards and who don't mind some major climbs and descents will enjoy the long ride. This route offers panoramas of Napa Valley, The Palisades, and Sugarloaf Mountain on the way to a 3,000-foot pass next to Mt. St. Helena. It's downhill to Middletown, followed by a short climb and descent into the sparsely populated Pope Valley. Returning to St. Helena you climb a steep ridge on Howell Mountain Road.

Rather than staying on busy Highway 29, take the secluded Lawley Road, built as a toll road in 1874 by John Lawley, an early pioneer and entrepreneur of the Napa Valley. Lawley had good business sense: When he built the road Mt. St. Helena was one giant mine shaft, with booming mining towns like Silverado on its slopes. Supply wagons and stage coaches had to take the steep, rocky Oat Hill Road between Calistoga and Middletown. When the railroad reached Calistoga in 1868, Lawley realized that a properly graded road would speed deliveries. Three years after opening the road he built the Toll House, a family residence, inn, and horse stable at the road's summit. The original house burned in 1883. A second house built at the same site burned in 1951. In 1923 the state purchased the toll road and built Highway 29, although the upper highway still follows Lawley Road.

Two well-known figures associated with Mt. St. Helena include writer Robert Louis Stevenson and bandit Black Bart. Stevenson, who wrote *Treasure Island, The Strange Case of Dr. Jekyll and Mr. Hyde,* and *Kidnapped,* lived on the mountain with his bride for one year in 1880. Their residence—a

12.2 Beware of train tracks.

14.4 Heitz Cellar winery on right.

14.5 Louis Martini winery on right.

14.8 Christian Brothers winery on right.

15.6 End ride on Pope Street.

Ride #2 Mountain Tour

0.0 Park in St. Helena on a side street. Start mileage at corner of Deer Park Road and Highway 29. Ride north on Highway 29 to Calistoga.

1.7 Old Bale Grist Mill State Park.

3.4 Bothe Napa Valley State Park.

6.8 **Right on Lincoln Avenue at stop sign (Highway 29) to downtown Calistoga.**

7.8 Silverado Trail junction on right.

▼

9.3 Right on Old Stage Road, also called Lawley Road. Begin steep 4.7-mile climb in .9 miles.

12.6 Right on Highway 29 at stop sign, continuing climb.

14.9 Summit. Robert Louis Stevenson State Park on left and hiking trail to Mt. St. Helena summit.

15.2 Unpaved service road to Mt. St. Helena summit, open to bicycles.

18.1 Lake County. Sprint!

23.8 Downtown Middletown. Food and drink.

24.4 Right on Butts Canyon Road at cemetery.

29.0 Oat Hill Road junction on right.

29.7 Deteret Reservoir.

35.5 Snell Valley Road junction on left. Begin 1.1-mile climb.

36.6 Summit. Begin 1.3-mile descent to Pope Valley.

miner's cabin—is gone, but you can still visit the site in Robert Louis Stevenson State Park by hiking one mile from the Highway 29 summit parking lot.

Charles Boles, alias Black Bart, also frequented the hills above Calistoga, robbing (with an unloaded gun) Wells Fargo stagecoaches traveling the toll road. His eight-year crime spree lasted until 1883. He spent his remaining years in San Quentin prison.

You can't miss Hubcap Ranch on Pope Valley Road, a recently dedicated state historic landmark. Litto Diamonte, an Italian immigrant, moved to the valley to farm in the early 1900s. His hubcap collection that started as a joke grew into thousands, until hubcaps covered the house and barn and lined the fences. Diamonte died in 1983, but his legacy shines on.

Pope Valley has a store where you can get food and drink before the final climb. It's closed Saturdays, however, as are all stores in the town of Angwin, built by Seventh Day Adventists. Near the end of the ride you'll get a chance to test your gears on Howell Mountain Road leading to Angwin. The two-mile ascent has a gradient between 9 and 13 percent.

38.4 Bridge over Pope Creek.

40.6 Hubcap Ranch.

42.9 Right on Howell Mountain Road in Pope Valley at stop sign. Begin steep 2.3-mile climb.

45.2 Summit.

46.7 Straight at College Avenue junction.

47.0 Town of Angwin.

48.9 Howell Mountain Road changes name to Deer Park Road at 4-way intersection.

52.8 Silverado Trail and stop sign.

53.5 End of ride at Highway 29. ∎

3. Muir Woods

Distance: **27 miles.**
Terrain: **Hilly.**
Traffic: **Cars, horses, hikers, bicyclists.**

Muir Woods is the site of stately redwoods in a canyon at the foot of Mt. Tamalpais. You'll visit this famous national monument on the Muir Woods ride and see the best that Marin County has to offer for scenic beauty and bicycling in Mt. Tamalpais State Park. The ride starts in Marin City along Richardson Bay, goes north through Mill Valley, skirts the rocky Pacific coast, and passes Muir Woods National Monument.

Mill Valley, the woodsy village at the base of Mt. Tamalpais, is home to a number of well-known artists and writers. The town's earliest settlers came here in the 1840s to log redwoods in the surrounding hills and work at a large sawmill on Old Mill Creek. In 1900 Mill Valley was incorporated, and thereafter became a playground for San Francisco's rich and famous, who delighted in riding the "Crookedest Railroad in the World" to the summit of Mt. Tamalpais (see Mt. Tamalpais off-road ride). Mill Valley experienced another growth boom when refugees of the 1906 earthquake and fire settled here.

You'll ride into town on Miller Avenue, which parallels the railroad right-of-way. The North Pacific Coast Railroad began train service to Mill Valley in 1890. Train service was replaced by buses in 1941. The train depot at Lytton Square was built in 1925 and was later converted to a book store and coffee shop.

Remnants of John Reed's sawmill are located in Old Mill Park next to Old Mill Creek. (Reed, an

Mileage Log

0.0 Start mileage at the parking area under Highway 101 in Marin City (to get there from Highway 101 northbound take the Highway 1 exit and turn right on Pohono Street, then turn left through an office building parking lot). Ride north on the recreation path.

0.2 Cross bridge over Coyote Creek.

0.7 Left onto Miller Avenue, which has a bike lane, at crosswalk.
▼

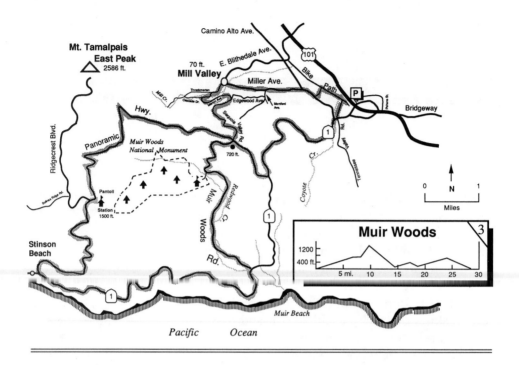

2.5 Left at stop sign on Throckmorton Avenue in downtown Mill Valley. To get there from Miller Avenue ride to the stop sign 15 yards away on your left. Turn right here to reach Throckmorton, next to the old train depot. Throckmorton runs east-west and is unsigned at the Miller intersection.

2.8 Left on Cascade Drive into Old Mill Park. Keep right at the next junction.

▼

early landowner in the area, established the first ferry service between Sausalito and San Francisco in the 1830s.) A roof was added to protect the timbers. Continue north through the park and begin climbing on Marion Avenue. This narrow concrete road winds past residences tucked away among the redwoods. By taking Marion Avenue you'll avoid the steep grades and heavy traffic on Edgewood Road, the main road to Panoramic Highway.

At Panoramic Highway you might be ready for something to drink. In the summer a vendor often sells fresh fruit and soda from a truck. Continue climbing on Panoramic Highway to the high point of the ride at 1,500 feet.

There's a water fountain at the Pan Toll ranger station and campsites nearby (reservations are required). Now it's all downhill to the ocean. On a hot day in the spring or fall Highway 1 becomes crowded with cars creeping to Stinson Beach starting from about a half-mile north of Panoramic

Highway. Early in the day traffic will be light going south. There's a grocery store at Stinson Beach.

The Coast Highway between Stinson Beach and Muir Beach Overlook follows a rocky shoreline with towering cliffs. The two-lane road has no shoulders, and in some locations you'll find uneven pavement caused by landslides along the unstable cliffs.

On Muir Woods Road traffic is light as you ride up the wide and scenic Frank Valley along Redwood Creek. The entrance to Muir Woods National Monument is located in Redwood Canyon at the beginning of a steep climb to Panoramic Highway. You must leave your bike outside before entering the park.

Marin County's remaining old-growth redwoods survive in Muir Woods thanks to the efforts of William Kent. Kent, a legislator who owned the only remaining land with old-growth (never cut) redwoods in Marin County, faced condemnation by a water company intent on building a reservoir. Kent's initial efforts to preserve the land by giving it to the government or having it declared a state park all failed, but eventually he learned of a little-known law that allowed valuable parcels of land to be turned into national monuments. In 1908, 295 acres were presented to the U.S. government and accepted by President Teddy Roosevelt. Kent asked that the monument be named after John Muir, who campaigned to make Yosemite Valley a national park. Today Muir Woods has more than one million visitors annually.

After descending Highway 1 you'll come to the busy Shoreline Highway. Follow the path back to the parking area under Highway 101, as described in the Mileage Log.

3.1 Left on Marion Avenue, uphill on a concrete road.

4.1 Right on Edgewood Avenue at stop sign. Edgewood becomes Sequoia Valley Road.

5.1 Right on Panoramic Highway at stop sign.

8.7 Left at Pan Toll park headquarters, staying on Panoramic Highway to Highway 1 Summit.

13.3 Left on Highway 1 at stop sign.

19.2 Left on Muir Woods Road.

21.7 Muir Woods National Monument. Bicycles not allowed in park. Water fountains and restrooms found in parking area.

23.4 Right on Panoramic Highway at stop sign. Summit.

24.3 Left on Highway 1 at stop sign, continuing descent to bay.

▼

26.8 Right on Highway 1 at traffic light. Ride about 200 yards, cross Coyote Creek bridge, and turn right on Tennessee Valley Road. Ride through gravel parking area on your right and walk or ride under bridge on a narrow path. Continue straight and pick up the paved recreation path beyond the bridge.

27.2 Right at path junction.

27.4 Finish at parking area under Highway 101.

■

Stinson Beach is a popular destination on warm spring days.

4. Point Reyes

Distance: **54 miles.**
Terrain: **Rolling or flat.**
Traffic: **Light to moderate.**

Fortunately much of Marin County has been protected as parkland; otherwise it might have become a victim of its own beauty. You'll more fully appreciate Marin County's scenery after taking this 54-mile ride that includes Point Reyes National Seashore, Samuel P. Taylor State Park, and the Marin County Watershed.

Fairfax, last in a chain of towns on Sir Francis Drake Boulevard, is a good place to start. You can park at the beginning of Bolinas Avenue in a parking lot between Sir Francis and Broadway. A block east on Broadway you'll see the Fairfax Theater, where the annual Thanksgiving Day mountain bike ride starts. Most of the cyclists who created the mountain bike live within riding distance, and many of them attend.

Bolinas Avenue becomes Fairfax–Bolinas Road as you cross San Anselmo Creek and climb the side of a canyon. Houses perched on poles cling to the canyon among toyons, bay laurels, poison oak, redwoods, and oaks. At the Meadow Club Golf Course and with an old barn on your right, there's a gate that may be closed on dry summer days when fire danger is high. Call the Water District to check on the road, (415) 924-4600.

From the first of two ridgetops you'll have a glimpse of Alpine Lake. (On your right is the fire road used for the Thanksgiving Day tour.) The Marin County watershed extends as far as the eye can see north, west, and south. After a nice descent

Mileage Log

0.0 Start mileage in Fairfax at parking lot between Sir Francis Drake Boulevard and Broadway at junction with Fairfax-Bolinas road. Ride south on Bolinas Avenue.

2.5 Meadow Club Golf Course.

3.7 Summit. Mountain bike rides take off from fire road on your right.

8.0 Cross Alpine Dam.

10.3 Right at stop sign. Summit.

14.6 Right on Highway 1 at stop sign.

15.2 Dogtown.

23.7 Olema.

▼

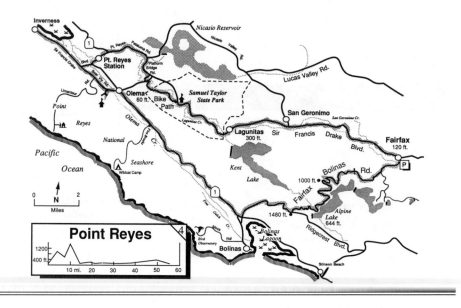

Point Reyes

23.8 Left on Bear Valley Road.

24.7 Left to Pt. Reyes National Seashore Park Headquarters. Return to Bear Valley Road and turn left.

26.7 Left on Sir Francis Drake Boulevard at stop sign.

27.2 Inverness Park.

29.8 Inverness. Return on Sir Francis Drake Boulevard to Highway 1, keeping left at the Bear Valley Road junction.

▼

on the two-lane road you'll wind through the redwoods to Alpine Lake dam, completed in 1919.

The road climbs steadily from the dam to Bolinas Ridge through redwoods and Douglas fir. Turn right at the T-intersection. There's a fire road on your right that's open to bicycles and that goes to Olema over the Bolinas Ridge Trail. Begin the descent to Highway 1. Watch out for poorly banked, bumpy corners.

For an interesting side trip go to the beach community of Bolinas and Bolinas Lagoon. You'll ride through a dense grove of eucalyptus west of Highway 1 where thousands of orange-and-black monarch butterflies often cluster in winter.

Otherwise turn right on Highway 1. The two-lane Coast Highway runs down the middle of the San Andreas Valley, rolling over short hills and through groves of eucalyptus and green pastures, where you'll see Pine Gulch Creek. The eucalyptus were planted here in the early 1900s. Don't miss the Dogtown sign (population 30) bolted to a eucalyptus tree.

Olema, nine miles away, is a convenient place to stop for a snack at one of several stores. It's a mile

Fairfax-Bolinas road at Alpine Lake is one of those mysterious-looking, winding roads that seems to beckon to bicyclists.

from here to the newly completed Pt. Reyes National Seashore headquarters. The building has a spacious interpretive center, restrooms, and water fountains.

Point Reyes used to be in Southern California but has drifted slowly north over the past 100 million years or so. Someday it will be in what is now Oregon. In 1962 about 64,000 acres were purchased for parkland, although ranchers still lease portions of the park for cattle grazing.

Bicyclists can reach the coast either by taking Fivebrooks to Stewart Trail or via the Coast Trail and Muddy Hollow Trail from Limantour Road.

Leave park headquarters on the same road and head north to Inverness. It's a flat ride, but you can expect headwinds. Inverness has numerous restaurants, and there's a good delicatessen at Inverness Park. Ride through Pt. Reyes Station and pick up Pt. Reyes-Petaluma Road about a half-mile outside

33.4 Left on Highway 1 at stop sign.

34.2 Ride through Pt. Reyes Station on Highway 1. Pt. Reyes Bikes, which has bike rentals available, is on your left on the north edge of town at 11431 Highway 1; (415) 663-1768.

34.5 Right on Pt. Reyes-Petaluma Road.

37.9 Right on Platform Bridge Road at stop sign.

▼

40.2 Right at bike route sign just before Sir Francis Drake Boulevard stop sign.

40.3 Left on bike path on other side of bridge.

42.5 Taylorville paper mill site.

43.5 Left over bridge to leave Samuel P. Taylor State Park at main entrance.

43.7 Right on Sir Francis Drake Boulevard at stop sign.

54.0 Fairfax.

■

town. On Platform Bridge Road you'll follow Lagunitas Creek to Sir Francis Drake Boulevard. Cross an old bridge before the stop sign and immediately turn left onto a beautiful paved recreation path. The path follows within feet of the tree-covered Lagunitas Creek, passing the site (with a marker and sign) of the first paper mill west of the Mississippi, built by Taylor himself in 1856. Taylorville, a company town and health resort, sprung up along the banks of the creek. The path was originally a railroad bed for the North Pacific Coast Railroad.

Leave the park through the main entrance, crossing a bridge over the creek. You're back on Sir Francis Drake Boulevard, which passes through Lagunitas, Forest Knolls, and San Geronimo on your return to Fairfax. The last 1.5 miles into town is a swift downhill.

5. Tiburon and Golden Gate

Distance: **31 miles.**
Terrain: **Mostly flat.**
Traffic: **Light to moderate.**

Tiburon, with its spectacular setting across the bay from highrise San Francisco, greets you like a picture postcard from the Marin County shoreline. By combining a bike ride with a ferry trip to Tiburon, Sausalito, or Angel Island you can tailor your trip to suit any fancy.

Start on the San Francisco side of Golden Gate Bridge. There's parking available in front of a cluster of concrete fortresses on Merchant Road, including Battery Boutelle, which was built in 1901 and decommissioned at the end of World War II. None of the guns at any of the forts at the Golden Gate were ever fired at an enemy.

The Golden Gate Bridge celebrated its 50th birthday on May 25, 1987, with extravagant fireworks and the installation of decorative lights to illuminate permanently the span's twin towers. More than 800,000 people (the heaviest load ever supported by the bridge) jammed onto the 8,940-foot span, which remained closed to traffic for six hours. Construction of the bridge took six years at a cost of $35 million and claimed the lives of 11 men. It was the longest suspension bridge at the time.

For your safety, obey these rules when crossing the bridge: You must ride on the west sidewalk on weekends and holidays, the east side on weekdays. Keep your speed down to 15 mph or less. Use caution, as it can be wet, cold, and windy any time of year. Iron gratings on the sidewalk are slippery when wet. Follow signs from the lot to a path

Mileage Log

0.0 Start mileage at coastal defense Battery Boutelle, on Merchant Road off Lincoln Boulevard and Highway 101. Ride east on Merchant Road.

0.1 **Left at tunnel entrance under Highway 101 and Golden Gate Bridge toll plaza. Ride through tunnel and turn left immediately after exiting.**

0.3 Ride over bridge on the east sidewalk weekdays, on the west sidewalk weekends.

2.0 Bridge ends. If on the east sidewalk ride into Vista Point parking lot, dismount and walk bike under Golden Gate Bridge stairway and path. Once you get to the west side walk back up stairs and ride downhill on paved road under the bridge. If you started on west side take first left through a gate and ride down road under bridge.

▼

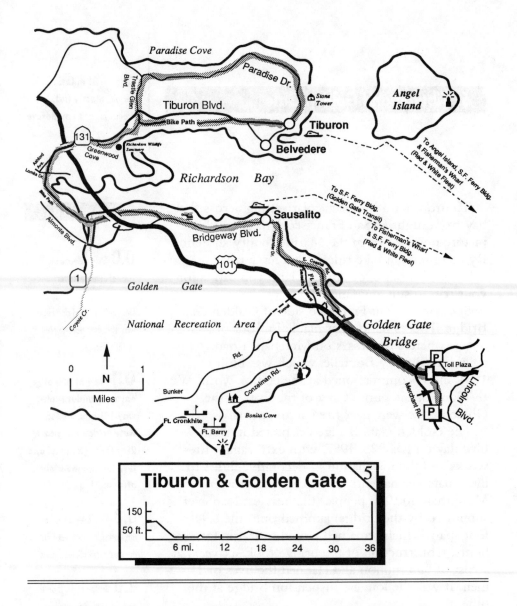

Tiburon & Golden Gate 5

2.8 **Right at stop sign. Ride through Fort Baker on Murray Circle.**

3.0 **Right on East Coastal Road.**
▼

under the bridge. It's an uphill ride the first half of the 1.7-mile span.

On the west side leave the bridge at a gate on your left and go down a steep paved road under the bridge. From the east side enter the Vista Point parking lot, walk your bike down wooden stairs to the sidewalk under the bridge, and ride from the parking lot down to the road under the bridge. At Fort Baker old army houses line a circular road where the Flying Wheels bicycle race was held for many years.

Sausalito is a quiet residential village on weekdays and a crowded tourist haven on weekends. In 1838 Captain William Richardson became one of the area's first residents. He purchased a 19,000-acre Mexican land grant called "Saucelito" and built an adobe house at what is now Pine and Bonita streets. By the turn of the century Sausalito was thriving, complete with ferry and rail terminal.

Sausalito transformed itself from a colorful resort town with big yachts into a bustling shipyard during World War II. In three years 93 freighters and tankers were built. More than 30,000 shipbuilders worked around the clock until Marinship shut down in late 1945. Local citizens want to build a Marinship museum next to the Army Corps of Engineers' Bay Model on Bridgeway. The Bay Model is a replica of San Francisco Bay that's the size of a two-acre warehouse. It was built by the U.S. Army Corps of Engineers as a hydraulic lab to study the bay. The model is open from 9 a.m. to 4 p.m., Tuesday through Saturday.

You're five miles into the ride now. You can turn back here and take a ferry to Fisherman's Wharf in San Francisco for less than $5, then cycle to your starting point (see San Francisco ride).

Wide, paved paths greet you most of the way to Tiburon. Pick up the path before Bridgeway merges with Highway 101. This is a right-of-way for the North Western Pacific Railroad. Houseboats next to the path are domesticated and have concrete foundations. Take the path underneath Highway 101's massive concrete columns and continue through the wetlands on the old railroad right-of-way.

Tiburon, a quiet residential alcove, was a busy rail terminal from 1884 until 1929. Peter Donahue, owner of the San Francisco and North Pacific Coast Railroad, expanded the narrow gauge line

3.8 Right before reaching tunnel, merging onto Alexander Drive.

3.9 Right at junction onto Bridgeway with double-yellow street reflectors.

4.5 Downtown Sausalito.

5.8 Bay Model museum and display on right.

6.8 Right onto bike path at freeway entrance and Gate Six Road.

7.6 Ride under Highway 101 overpass on path.

7.8 Cross bridge going north. Drinking fountain at mile 9.1.

9.2 Path ends. Begin East Blithedale Avenue at traffic light.

9.8 Highway 101 overpass. East Blithedale becomes Tiburon Boulevard.

10.6 Right on Greenwood Cove at traffic light. Take first left after right turn. Name changes to Greenwood Beach.

▼

11.0 Richardson Bay Audubon Society Center and Sanctuary.

11.5 **Right on path at end of Greenwood Beach. Portable toilets at mile 11.6. Drinking fountain at mile 11.9.**

13.7 Path ends. Ride into Tiburon on Main Street.

13.8 Downtown Tiburon.

14.0 Ferry dock for San Francisco and Angel Island. Golden Gate Transit (415) 453-2100 or Red & White Fleet (415) 546-2815. Paradise Drive begins from ferry building.

14.4 Lyford Stone Tower.

17.3 Paradise Beach Park. Bicycles pay $1 to enter. Portable toilet, drinking fountains.

19.3 **Left on Trestle Glen Boulevard.**

19.9 Cross Tiburon Boulevard at traffic light and pick up path.

20.0 **Left onto Greenwood Beach. Retrace route.**

through Marin, Sonoma, and Napa counties with the help of his son James. You're about 14 miles from the Golden Gate. You can take the ferry to Angel Island or San Francisco, or continue on beautiful Paradise Drive. Angel Island has a paved path circling its perimeter.

Paradise Drive rolls gently around the peninsula, passing the Lyford Stone Tower. The tower was built in 1889 by San Francisco architect Gustav Behrnd for Dr. Benjamin F. Lyford, an embalming surgeon during the Civil War who moved West to regain his health at Tiburon. Lyford, who made his fortune by being the first person to use makeup on corpses, lived in a Victorian house on Greenwood Beach Road, easily identified by its bright yellow paint. It's now part of the Richardson Bay Wildlife Sanctuary and open to the public.

On the eastern shore of the peninsula, Paradise Beach County Park provides a good rest stop with a view of San Pablo Strait. There's a restroom, picnic tables, a pier, and barbecue pits. An entry fee is required of all visitors.

Complete the peninsula loop by turning left on Trestle Glen Road and descending to Tiburon Boulevard. Retrace your route to complete the ride.

20.9 **Left on Tiburon Boulevard at Greenwood Cove traffic light.**

21.8 Highway 101 overpass.

22.2 **Right on Ashford Street (for easier access to recreation path).**

22.4 **Left on Lomita Drive at stop sign.**

22.6 **Cross East Blithedale at traffic light and pick up path on right.**

24.2 Ride under Highway 101.

24.9 Sausalito Cyclery, open 7 days a week.

25.0 **Left on Bridgeway from Gate Six Road.**

▼

Lyford Stone Tower near Tiburon was built in 1889 for Dr. Benjamin F. Lyford.

27.0 Downtown Sausalito.

27.9 Fort Baker exit on right if you choose to return this route. Or go straight as follows:

28.7 Left on recreation path.

29.0 View Point parking area.

29.1 Enter Golden Gate Bridge sidewalk.

30.8 End bridge.

30.9 Take tunnel under toll booths.

31.0 Right on Merchant Road at stop sign.

31.1 End ride.

■

6. Atherton and Edgewood Park

0.0 Start mileage at the intersection of Fair Oaks and Station lanes in Atherton. Permit parking is available next to the train station (50 cents). Ride west on Fair Oaks.

0.2 Cross El Camino Real at traffic light and continue straight on Atherton Avenue.

2.0 **Right on Alameda de las Pulgas Avenue at stop sign.**

3.0 Cross Highway 84 at traffic light.

3.2 **Left on Fernside Street, the first left after crossing 84.**

4.3 **Road ends. Turn left on McGarvey Avenue.**

▼

It would be easy for an Atherton resident to forget that the San Francisco peninsula is anything but rural countryside: this exclusive community consists largely of palatial estates hidden behind tall walls and impressive oak trees. On this tour you'll ride through rural and entirely residential Atherton to Edgewood Park in the foothills above Redwood City. Edgewood Park is known for its display of wildflowers in the spring. Several plants and butterflies in the park are rare and endangered species. Plans for a golf course in the park that would have threatened the plants' and butterflies' habitat were abandoned in 1988.

Your ride begins at the Atherton train station on the east side of Highway 82, El Camino Real. Leave the parking lot and ride west to El Camino Real on the tree-shaded Fair Oaks Lane. El Camino became a major route in the late 1700s when it was used by Spanish settlers to travel between the San Francisco Presidio and missions to the south. Cross El Camino where the road becomes Atherton Avenue. Stay on Atherton until Alameda de las Pulgas, Spanish for "Avenue of the Fleas."

Atherton was named for Faxon Atherton, a prosperous hide and tallow trader from Chile who traveled in California during the 1830s. The town was called Fair Oaks until 1912. Mansions were built on the level oak-covered land by wealthy San Franciscans seeking an escape to the country and the valley's warmth on cold, foggy days. The train was a popular means of travel in the early days. In 1864 the 28-mile ride from San Francisco took one hour and 15 minutes, only a bit longer than it takes by train today.

Millionaires like mining magnate James Claire Flood and Mark Hopkins, one of the "Big Four" of the Central Pacific Railroad in the 1870s, had summer homes here. Other prominent Atherton residents included Thomas Selby, an industrialist who made his fortune smelting precious metals, W.E. Barron, an owner of the New Almaden mercury mines, and baseball greats Ty Cobb and Willie Mays.

Turn right on Alameda de las Pulgas and head north along residential streets to Jefferson Avenue. You'll have a steady climb on Jefferson Avenue for about one mile. At the top of Jefferson turn right on California Way at the Emerald Lake Fire Station. The climbing ends when you reach the park. There's a service road through Edgewood, but it was closed to bicycles in 1988.

Retrace your route to Jefferson and turn right. (Turn right from Jefferson Avenue and ride north 1.5 miles if you want to see the impressive Filoli Center gardens and the Pulgas Water Temple.) Take Cañada Road to Woodside. Cañada Road is closed to cars and open for bicycling every first and third Sunday, April through October, between Edgewood Road and Highway 92 (9 a.m. to 4 p.m.).

Continue straight at Highway 84 onto the narrow, shaded Mountain Home Road. You'll cross Dry Creek and then Bear Gulch Creek before turning left onto Manzanita Way. Manzanita was one of the bumpiest roads in the world until it was repaved in 1987. Stop and look both directions at the Sand Hill Road intersection before turning left. You'll be greeted by a gradual climb, with an equestrian dressage arena on the left and a Christmas tree farm on the right. A scene from the movie *Harold and Maude* was filmed at the hilltop to the left.

Cross Interstate 280 and descend to Santa Cruz Avenue. Turn left at the traffic light, keeping left at

4.4 Right on Farm Hill Boulevard at traffic light.

4.7 Left on Jefferson Avenue at traffic light.

6.4 Right on California Way at Emerald Lake fire station and church.

6.8 Right on Sunset Way. Continue on Sunset, which turns to dirt.

7.2 Cross Hillcrest on Robertson Way and enter Edgewood Park at gate. Return to Jefferson Avenue by same route.

7.9 Right on Jefferson Avenue at stop sign.

8.8 Left on Cañada Road at stop sign.

10.5 Cross Highway 84 intersection at stop sign and continue straight on Mountain Home Road.

10.9 Left on Manzanita Way.

12.2 Left on Sand Hill Road at stop sign.
▼

15.3 Left on Santa Cruz Avenue at traffic light.

15.4 Bear left to Alameda de las Pulgas, at the junction with Santa Cruz Avenue, where there's a traffic light.

16.9 Right on Atherton Avenue at stop sign.

18.7 Cross El Camino Real and go straight on Fair Oaks Lane.

18.9 End of ride at Atherton train station.

■

the next traffic light where Santa Cruz Avenue joins Alameda de las Pulgas. There's a neighborhood shopping center with a pizza parlor, delicatessen, gas station, and grocery store a short distance beyond the traffic light. Continue north on Alameda de las Pulgas and turn right on Atherton Avenue to retrace your route to the train depot.

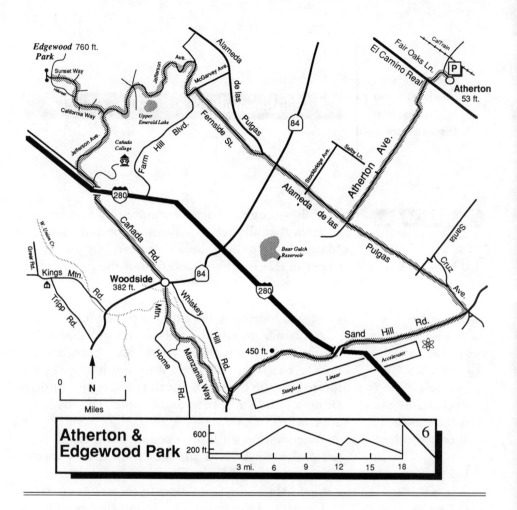

Edgewood 760 ft. Park

Sunset Way

Haven Way

California Way

Jefferson Ave.

Jefferson Ave.

Upper Emerald Lake

Cañada College

Farm Hill Blvd.

Fernside St.

McGarvey Ave.

Alameda de las Pulgas

84

El Camino Real

Fair Oaks Ln.

CalTrain

P

Atherton 53 ft.

Atherton Ave.

Selby Ln.

Stockbridge Ave.

Alameda de las Pulgas

Bear Gulch Reservoir

Santa Cruz Ave.

280

W. Union Cr.

Greer Rd.

Kings Mtn. Rd.

Tripp Rd.

Cañada Rd.

84

Woodside 382 ft.

Whiskey Hill Rd.

Mtn.

Home Rd.

Manzanita Way

280

Sand Hill Rd.

450 ft. ●

Stanford Linear Accelerator

0   1

N

Miles

Atherton & Edgewood Park

600

200 ft.

3 mi.   6   9   12   15   18

6

Distance: **13 miles.**
Terrain: **One long hill, two short hills.**
Traffic: **Light to moderate.**

7. Hillsborough

Mileage Log

0.0 Start mileage at the intersection of East Fifth Avenue and South B Street in downtown San Mateo. Talbot's Bike Shop is located on the corner. Four-hour parking on weekdays available on South Railroad Avenue next to the Caltrain tracks and parking lot. No time limit on weekends. Ride west on Fifth Avenue.

0.1 Japanese garden and tennis courts at left on Laurel Avenue. Follow path through park to see garden behind high wooden fence.

0.5 **Right on Dartmouth Road at giant bay tree and stop sign.**

0.6 Dartmouth jogs left.
▼

Hillsborough is a stately community tucked away in the hills between Burlingame and San Mateo. For a million dollars you can buy a fixer-upper in this neighborhood (minus the gardener, of course). But for a more modest investment in time and energy you can enjoy this beautiful peninsula location without paying the rent.

A 12-mile grand tour of Hillsborough's estates begins in downtown San Mateo. Start near Talbot's, a well-known bicycle store and hobby shop located on the corner of South B Street and Fifth. Bring a good street map on this ride: The roads are hard to follow.

Ride west on Fifth for a couple of blocks, turn left on Laurel Avenue, and then immediately turn right into Central Park. There's a beautiful Japanese garden behind the fence, next to the tennis courts.

Return to Fifth, cross El Camino Real heading west, and take a right at the next stop sign on Dartmouth Road, where there's a huge bay tree across the street. Dartmouth jogs left in one block; cross Third Avenue at the stop light. Continue straight for a block to Arroyo Court, site of the first Gaspar de Portola expedition. The captain and his men camped here in 1769, a few days after discovering San Francisco Bay.

Turn left on Arroyo Court and go about 70 yards to the end of the street. Take the short footpath to Crystal Springs Road and cross the bridge over San Mateo Creek. Crystal Springs Road takes you to Skyline Boulevard, which follows San

Mateo Creek gently uphill. Numerous shell mounds left by the coastal Indians have been found along the creek. At Polhemus Road, you'll branch right and begin a steeper climb of nearly a mile to Skyline. Polhemus Road is named for Charles Polhemus, a director of the Southern Pacific Railroad in the 1860s who helped build San Mateo.

You'll see two spectacular sights during the climb. The first is the four massive concrete pillars that support the Interstate 280 Doran Bridge spanning San Mateo Creek. The second is Crystal Springs Dam; look for it below the bridge. It was an impressive site when completed in 1887, then the largest concrete dam in the world. The dam was so well built that it withstood the 1906 earthquake without a crack.

At Skyline Boulevard you can either turn right or lengthen the ride by riding straight on Sawyer Camp Road, behind the gate (see Casual Rides).

You'll have 1.3 miles of climbing on Skyline until you turn right on Golf Course Drive and ride under Interstate 280. After a brisk descent on Ralston Road, you'll turn left and enter the exclusive Burlingame Country Club and Golf Course. President Teddy Roosevelt visited the club while campaigning in 1903. Founded in 1892 (at a different site) by San Francisco socialites, the club attracts the peninsula's rich and famous.

The road through the golf course is lined with magnificent white-bark eucalyptus. Stay on Eucalyptus until Forest View Avenue. Turn right and ride between 50-foot-high cypress lining the road.

The road winds around the golf course and heads south, becoming Sharon Road and then Hillsborough Boulevard. Sharon Road is named for Senator William Sharon of Nevada, one of the early town builders on the peninsula. There's a short, steep climb before you begin descending. You'll find the oldest and grandest of the Hillsborough estates at the bottom of the hill.

Hillsborough was incorporated in 1910. To

0.7 Left on Arroyo Court. Ride to end of court and take dirt path on right 10 yards up to bridge and Crystal Springs Road. Cross road with caution.

0.8 Ride west on Crystal Springs Road.

1.6 Keep left on Crystal Springs Road at El Cerrito Avenue junction. Crystal Springs Road follows San Mateo Creek.

3.3 Crystal Springs Road jogs right at Polhemus Road junction. Begin climb to Skyline.

4.0 Ride under Interstate 280.

4.2 Right on Skyline Boulevard at stop sign.

5.5 Right on Golf Course Drive at stop sign. Ride under Interstate 280.

5.6 Go straight. Hayne Road begins after stop sign.

5.7 Ride around circle and continue north on Darrell Road.

▼

5.8 **Right on Ralston Avenue.**

6.9 Keep right at Provident Drive.

7.9 **Left on Eucalyptus Avenue at stop sign.**

8.0 Eucalyptus jogs right through Burlingame Country Club golf course. Ride through grove of white eucalyptus.

8.6 **Right on Forest View Avenue and ride through tall cypress.**

8.9 Keep right on Sharon Road.

9.2 Sharon becomes Hillsborough Boulevard.

10.5 **Left at stop sign on West Santa Inez Avenue. Begin descent.**

10.8 Stop sign. Stay on Santa Inez.

11.0 **Keep right. Road becomes Roblar Avenue.**

maintain its privacy the town annexed eight square miles all the way to Crystal Springs Dam and does not permit business.

11.5 **Left on El Cerrito Avenue at stop sign. El Cerrito becomes Tilton Avenue east of El Camino.**

12.1 **Right on North B Street at stop sign.**

12.6 **Left on Fifth Avenue. End of ride.**

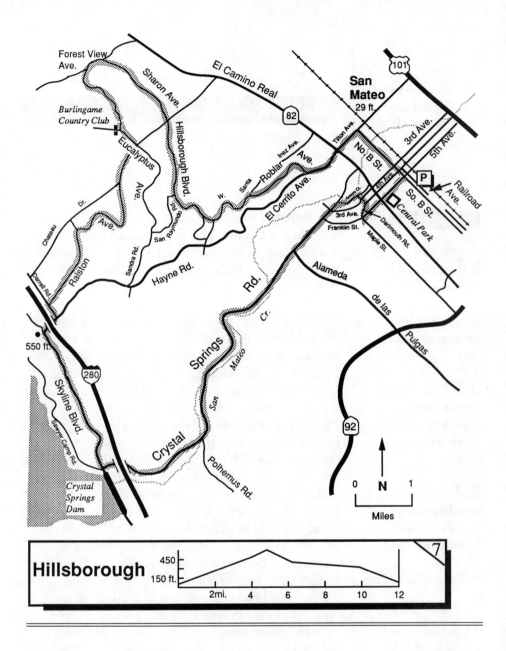

Hillsborough

8. San Bruno Mountain

Mileage Log

0.0 Start mileage at the intersection of Linden Avenue and Hillside Boulevard. A grocery store is located nearby. Ride west on Hillside through Colma.

3.8 **Right on Market Street at bottom of hill at traffic light. Becomes Guadalupe Canyon Parkway.**

5.7 **Left into San Bruno Mountain Park. Circle back under Guadalupe Parkway.**

6.0 Start climb up Radio Road.

7.6 Parking lot for transmission towers and TV 38. Go back same way.

▼

South San Francisco and Colma have always lived in the shadow of San Francisco. But a closer look at each of these communities reveals a mountain known for both its beautiful displays of wildflowers in the spring and its breathtaking summit views of the Bay Area and the Farallon Islands.

You can start your ride anywhere at the base of the mountain, but a clockwise direction is recommended to avoid left turns and freeway ramps. A hodgepodge of industrial parks, cemeteries, rolling hills, residential areas, the bay, and a lagoon lie along the route. Riding on the little-used Old Bayshore Boulevard early Sunday morning, a stone's throw from Highway 101, it's difficult to imagine that this was the southern gateway to San Francisco until the early 1960s when the freeway opened.

The fragile beauty of San Bruno Mountain has not gone unnoticed: It has long been the focus of a bitter struggle between developers and conservationists. The mountain's habitat supports two endangered butterfly species (San Bruno Elfin and Callippe Silverspot) and 14 species of rare or endangered plants. A prolonged battle ultimately resulted in the creation of a 2,326 acre park and a citizens' group called Save San Bruno Mountain, devoted to preserving the open space. In 1978 San Mateo County and the state purchased 1,500 acres and additional acreage was donated. The mountain now has 12 miles of hiking trails.

One of the more unusual places in the Bay Area is Hillside Boulevard through the town of Colma,

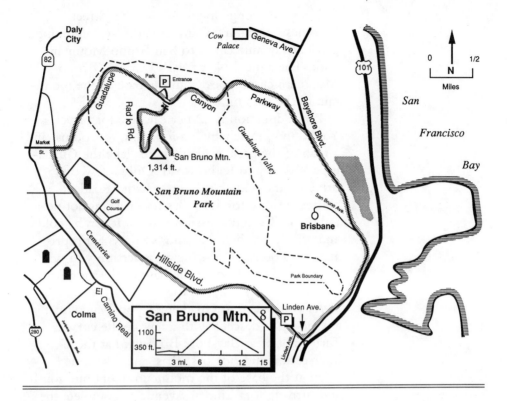

where the dead outnumber the living by at least 2,000 to 1. In the late 1800s, Colma was a thriving agricultural town producing artichokes, flowers, cauliflower, potatoes, turnips, and strawberries. But in the 1890s the character of the land changed dramatically when farm plots began to be replaced by burial plots. Colma secured its place as a burial center when San Francisco banned any more burials within its city limits in 1907. The Catholic Holy Cross Cemetery, founded in 1887, became the first of more than a dozen cemeteries. At least a million people are buried here, including newspaper publisher William Randolph Hearst and gunfighter Wyatt Earp. Colma, which wasn't incorporated until 1941, has 500 living residents. Near Olivet Memorial Park on the north side of Hillside there's even a pet cemetery. Farmers grow flowers rather than food at the base of the mountain.

9.4 Left on Guadalupe Canyon Parkway at stop sign.

11.5 Right on Bayshore Boulevard at traffic light.

14.2 Right on Linden Avenue at traffic light.

14.4 Right on Hillside Boulevard at traffic light. End of ride.

■

If you're riding clockwise, Market Street becomes Guadalupe Canyon Parkway, beginning a gradual 1.8-mile climb to San Bruno Mountain Park. The annual New Year's Day San Bruno Mountain climb goes from the base of the mountain to the summit.

Park admission is $2 per car, free for bicycles. You'll find picnic tables, a fountain, restrooms, and a map of the park available here. Take the Guadalupe Parkway to Radio Road. Only a few cars drive up the wide but bumpy Radio Road. It climbs steadily for 1.4 miles to a parking lot near radio and TV transmission towers. It can be cold and windy on the mountain, so dress appropriately. On occasion, during an inversion you will find it cold and hazy at the base of the mountain but warm and sunny on top.

As you return to Guadalupe, you'll encounter a wide-open descent with a few gentle curves. Turn right onto Bayshore Boulevard at the T-intersection and ride past Brisbane, a secluded town at the base of the mountain. Continue south and turn right at Linden Avenue to complete the loop.

9. Old LaHonda Road

Distance: **39 miles.**
Terrain: **Hilly.**
Traffic: **Light.**

Old LaHonda Road, one of the most secluded roads in San Mateo County, is popular with bicyclists riding from Portola Valley to Skyline Boulevard. Although the climb is steeper than Highway 84 to the north, there's little traffic on the narrow road hidden beneath a canopy of bay laurels, oaks, and redwoods.

This ride starts in Woodside, a forested community known for its stately mansions and horse ranches. The town got its start in the mid-1800s as a cluster of stores and hotels serving the drivers of wagons carrying logs to the port of Redwood City. Today town roads serve cars, bicycles, and horseback riders on busy weekends. Ride carefully and obey all traffic laws.

Old LaHonda Road was one of the earliest roads in the area built for logging. It was extended to LaHonda in 1876 and made a toll road, called the Redwood City and Pescadero Turnpike. The road's course has changed little over the years.

Leave Woodside and ride south on Mountain Home Road, where there's a gentle climb before a descent to Portola Road. Palatial estates are hidden behind tan oak, eucalyptus, scotch broom, and redwoods. The road was built in 1872 to link Woodside with Searsville, a once thriving community now covered by Searsville Lake. Portola Road cuts across the lake's marshy backwater.

On the left, at the junction of Portola and Old LaHonda roads, you'll see the oldest vineyard in the

Mileage Log

0.0 Start mileage at Woodside School on Highway 84, .2 miles west of downtown Woodside. Ride east on Highway 84.

0.2 Right on Mountain Home Road at 4-way stop.

0.6 Manzanita Road on left.

2.2 Left on Portola Road at stop sign.

2.4 Right on Portola Road at stop sign.

2.8 Right on Old LaHonda Road. Begin 3.4-mile climb.

6.2 Skyline Boulevard. Cross road and continue on Old LaHonda Road. Begin descent.

▼

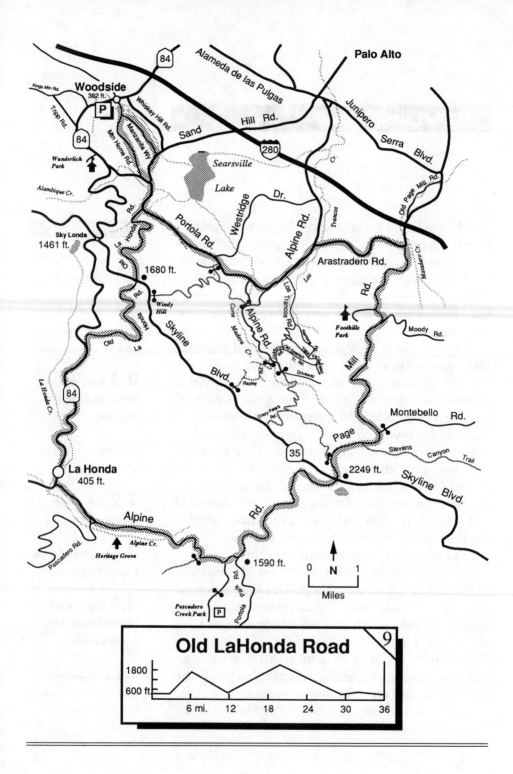

Old LaHonda Road

9

1800					
600 ft					
	6 mi.| 12	18	24	30	36

Old LaHonda Road in San Mateo County was built in the mid-1800s.

8.8 Left on Highway 84 at stop sign. Stop, look, and listen before crossing at blind corner.

12.0 LaHonda. Grocery store and restaurant on right in shopping center.

12.7 Left on Pescadero Road.

13.8 Continue straight onto Alpine Road in the redwoods. 5.6-mile climb begins at mile 14.8.

17.5 Entrance to Honor Camp and Pescadero Creek Park on right.

17.9 Left at stop sign. Right goes to Portola State Park.

21.3 Skyline Boulevard. Cross and continue on Page Mill Road.

22.0 Alpine Road on left behind green gate. Dirt road for 2.7 miles connects with paved Alpine Road.

27.1 Keep left at junction with Moody Road.

▼

area, dating back to the 1870s. A few vineyards can still be found around Woodside.

Some interesting historical features are to be found at the base of Old LaHonda Road. Preston Road on the right was actually Portola Road until the road alignment was changed. Next, watch for a concrete stairway on your right less than 50 yards after crossing Dennis Martin Creek. It is all that's left of the main house of a lavishly landscaped 300-acre estate owned by August Schilling, the famous spice mogul, and was torn down in 1953. The original guest house is on the right at the bottom of the hill. Millionaire Edgar Preston built the mansion in the 1870s. And finally, the driveway straight ahead at the first hairpin turn crossing Dennis Martin Creek is the old Dennis Martin Road, the scene of some of the earliest logging in the Santa Cruz Mountains.

About two miles into the climb there's a steep right bend in the road where, in the stage coach days, passengers had to disembark and walk—or push the wagon—to more level ground. As you reach the summit the redwood forest becomes so dense that the road is dark.

Cross Skyline Boulevard to begin the descent. Skyline, called "Wonder Way" when conceived in 1917, was built between 1920 and '29 and extends 47 miles south from San Francisco.

Old LaHonda Road on the west slope wasn't paved until 1987. Turn left on Highway 84 at the stop sign. Listen carefully for traffic at this blind corner. It may be safer to backtrack on Highway 84 before crossing. Traffic is heavy on the wide two-lane highway on hot weekends when Bay Area residents flock to the beaches. Most days traffic is light, however, and the descent to the rustic town of LaHonda is fun. At times there's a dramatic drop in temperature approaching LaHonda: On some winter days it's so cold here you feel like you're riding into a meat locker.

Turn left on Pescadero Road after riding through LaHonda and continue straight onto Alpine Road

Alpine Road, here shown looking west, two miles from Skyline Boulevard, leads to the heart of redwood country.

at the bridge. Shortly you'll pass a grove of old redwoods, known as Heritage Grove, on the right along Alpine Creek. The grove was saved from logging in the late 1960s when it became part of Sam McDonald County Park. Trees originally designated to get the ax still have blue paint marks.

Alpine Road climbs steadily to Skyline Boulevard with gradients between 8 and 12 percent. Once past Portola State Park Road you'll see impressive views of the coast and the Santa Cruz Mountains.

Cross Skyline Boulevard at the summit and proceed on Page Mill Road. William Page, who was a gold miner before he became a woodsman, built the road to his mill in Portola State Park in 1866. The road was called the Mayfield and Pescadero Road at the time. Page was interested in the most direct route, and damn the horses. Some gradients are between 15 and 18 percent. Passengers taking

27.3 Entrance to Foothills Park. Drinking fountain outside gate.

29.6 Left on Arastradero Road.

31.6 Left on Alpine Road at stop sign.

32.8 Right on Portola Road at stop sign.

36.1 Portola Road on left.
▼

36.8 Left on Manzanita Way near bottom of hill.

38.1 Right on Mountain Home Road at stop sign.

38.5 Left on Highway 84 at stop sign.

38.7 End of ride at Woodside School.

■

the stage coach to Pescadero for a vacation no doubt had a thrilling journey.

About a half-mile from Skyline Boulevard, Alpine Road intersects Page Mill on the left behind a green gate. The road is dirt for 2.6 miles and is popular for its mild grade.

Page Mill's steepest section begins midway at a hairpin turn called Shotgun Bend, which got its name because it was a popular spot for target practice before being incorporated by Palo Alto. Farther down you'll pass Moody Road on the right, another former logging road, and in a short distance Foothills Park on the left, where there's a drinking fountain near the road.

Turn left on Arastradero Road at the bottom of Page Mill and return to Woodside through Portola Valley on Alpine, Portola and Mountain Home roads.

10. Pescadero Road

Distance: **28 miles.**
Terrain: **Rolling hills.**
Traffic: **Light.**

The remote southwestern corner of San Mateo County has changed only marginally in the past century. You can still find remote wooded canyons with pristine streams, redwood forests, and acres of farmland here. This is an ideal tour for escaping the hectic pace of the Bay Area: You'll follow the old coast highway, see the villages of Pescadero and San Gregorio, and ride through redwoods along wooded creeks.

The ride begins in the town of Pescadero only a mile from the coast, making a loop out of Stage Road, Highway 84, and Pescadero Road. In 1870 Pescadero resembled a New England community, says author Alan Hynding in his book *From Frontier to Suburb.* It had almost 400 residents, white one- and two-storey buildings, and neatly plowed farmlands. A thriving lumber industry upstream on Pescadero Creek helped maintain the town's four stores, livery stables, and two hotels. Later dairy farming became the town's mainstay. Today Pescadero retains a friendly farming town charm.

Leave town heading north on Stage Road, the old coast highway, passing the white-steepled church on the left and two cemeteries on the right, one Catholic, one Protestant. It's six miles to the next junction at San Gregorio.

You'll ride through a long valley with eucalyptus trees on the left and grazing cattle in open meadows. Song birds can be heard among willows beside the road. In a few miles you'll ride under a canopy of giant eucalyptus at the end of which is

Mileage Log

0.0 Start mileage at the intersection of Stage Road and Pescadero Road in Pescadero. Ride north on Stage Road.

0.1 North Street on right.

2.4 Begin first 1-mile climb on Stage Road.

4.5 Begin final .8-mile climb on Stage Road.

7.1 Right on Highway 84 at stop sign. Restrooms across the road at Peterson and Alsford Store.

14.6 Right on Pescadero Road and green sign to Sam McDonald Park.

▼

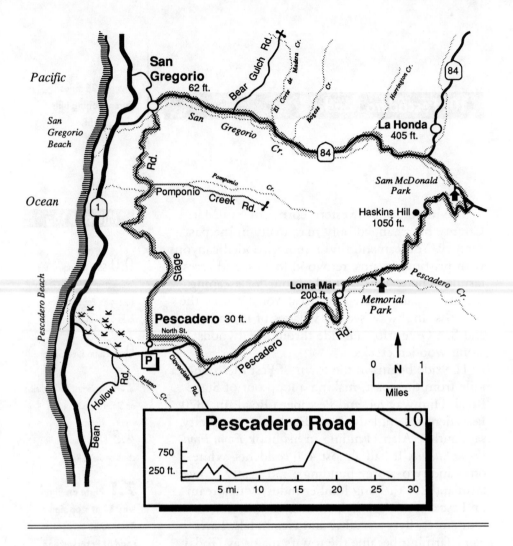

Pescadero Road 10

Pacific

San Gregorio 62 ft.

San Gregorio Beach

Ocean

Pescadero Beach

La Honda 405 ft.

Sam McDonald Park

Haskins Hill 1050 ft.

Pomponio Creek Rd.

Loma Mar 200 ft.

Memorial Park

Pescadero 30 ft.

North St.

Bean Hollow Rd.

Butano Cr.

Cloverdale Rd.

Pescadero Rd.

Stage Rd.

Bear Gulch Rd.

El Corte de Madera Cr.

Burgess Cr.

Harrington Cr.

Pescadero Cr.

0 N 1

Miles

750

250 ft.

5 mi. 10 15 20 25 30

15.7 **Right to stay on Pescadero Road at Alpine Road junction. Begin 1.6-mile climb.**

16.3 Sam McDonald County Park entrance. Restrooms and water.

▼

the large white house of the Willowside Farm (a former dairy). You may hear the piercing call of peacocks that live on the farm.

You'll begin a steady mile-long climb with a hayfield on the left as you leave the valley. The brown metal shed in the middle of the field is used for testing electronic equipment that must be isolated from radio waves. At the summit you'll have a panorama of the road winding down to Pomponio Creek and then up the next ridge. It's a mile down and a mile up. During the climbs you'll see

Stage Road north of Pescadero offers car-free cycling in a bucolic setting.

Stage Road looking north to Pomponio Creek has two mile-long grades.

17.3 Haskins Hill summit.

19.9 Entrance to Memorial Park. Restrooms and water.

21.3 Loma Mar Store. Portable toilet, water, food.

25.1 Pumpkin tree on right in front of house and next to hedge.

25.8 Butano Cutoff Road on left.

26.3 Phipps Ranch on left.

▼

the coast to the left. The next mile-long descent leads to a bridge over San Gregorio Creek and past the old stagecoach stop on the left at Highway 84. Cross the two-lane highway and stop for a visit at the Peterson and Alsford Store, where you can get warm in front of a wood-burning stove on cold days or have a cold drink in the summer at their authentic Old West bar. It's a popular resting place for bicyclists and travelers.

Return to Highway 84 and ride east up a wide, flat agricultural valley. Typically you'll have a tailwind from the coastal breeze and headwinds farther inland. The road climbs gradually as you follow San Gregorio Creek. Along the way you'll cross El Corte de Madera, Bogess, and Harrington creeks before reaching the forest and the outskirts of LaHonda.

About a quarter-mile from where you'll turn right, look for a large yellow log cabin on the right in a clearing under the redwoods. This was once the home of Ken Kesey, author of *One Flew Over the Cookoo's Nest*.

Turn right at the large green sign for Sam McDonald County Park. There's a mile of level riding through majestic redwoods before a two-mile climb from the Alpine Creek bridge. Pescadero Road was built by the county in 1876 and opened a year later. You'll pass park headquarters on the right in a half-mile, where there's water and restrooms.

At the top of Haskins Hill there's a view of Butano Ridge to the south as you begin a long, sweeping descent to Memorial Park and Loma Mar. At the Loma Mar store there's a lounge with a television, pool table, fireplace, and tables outside where you can soak up the sun on warm days. From Loma Mar you'll continue along Pescadero Creek through the redwoods. If you're riding here in autumn, watch for a tree hung with small pumpkins; it's on the right, in front of a house.

The road emerges from the canyon into flat farmland with Pescadero High School on the left. You'll pass a fruit stand and blackberry farm where you can pick your own. It's a mile-and-a-half to Pescadero from the farm.

26.5 Right on North Street.

27.4 Left on Stage Road at stop sign.

27.5 End of ride in town.

■

11. Portola Valley

0.0 Start mileage on Stanford University campus next to Stanford Stadium on Galvez Street. There's plenty of parking available next to Angell Field at Eucalyptus Drive.

0.1 Left on Campus Drive East at stop sign.

1.7 Right on Junipero Serra Boulevard at traffic light.

2.1 Campus Drive West intersection.

2.7 Left on Alpine Road at traffic light.

5.7 Arastradero Road intersection. Alpine Inn on left.

6.9 Right on Portola Road at stop sign.

▼

Overlooked by the forested Coast Range, Portola Valley is one of the most popular and scenic locations for riding in San Mateo County. On this route, called "The Loop" by local cyclists, you'll see Stanford University, equestrian parks, orchards, and the Stanford Linear Accelerator, a center for atomic particle research.

This ride starts at Stanford University stadium on Galvez Street. You'll ride through the attractive campus with its 19th century sandstone architecture and then turn north on Junipero Serra Boulevard, a busy two-lane road. The road crosses San Francisquito Creek at Alpine Road.

The origins of Alpine Road date back to the Costanoan Indians, who used a route just south of here to travel between the bay and ocean. In 1839 Antonio Buelna became the first recorded settler in Portola Valley and continued using the path for horse and wagon. Back then it was called Old Spanish Trail.

The road has a wide shoulder and the Dwight F. Crowder Memorial Bicycle Path on the south side; it's narrow and bumpy and has a lot of foot traffic. Yield at driveways and intersections if you ride on the path.

Beyond a residential neighborhood on your left you'll pass an equestrian park and a small farm that sells locally grown produce, followed by Interstate 280 and Ladera Shopping Center. The road climbs gradually as it parallels Los Trancos Creek, passing meadows, oak-covered hills, a few residences, a

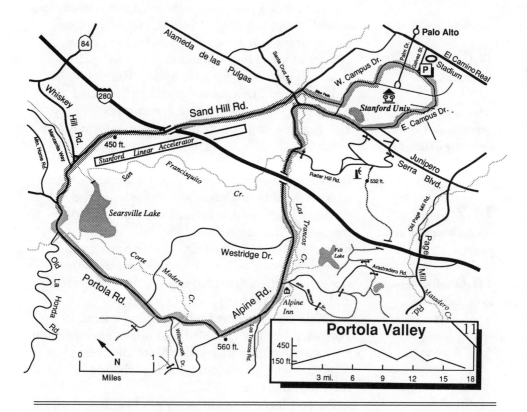

country club, and baseball and soccer fields. Coyotes, foxes, and bobcats are occasionally seen from the road. At the intersection with Arastradero Road there's Alpine Inn, known to locals as Rossotti's. It was established as a tavern for thirsty loggers in 1840 and draws mostly Stanford students, ranchers, farmers, and bicyclists today. Hamburgers and beer are the standard fare to be enjoyed outdoors on long picnic tables.

If you stay on Alpine Road instead of turning right at Portola Road, it climbs gradually through

9.7 Old LaHonda Road intersection on left.

10.3 Continue straight on Sand Hill Road where Portola Road goes left.

10.9 Manzanita Way intersection on left.

▼

11.0 Whiskey Hill Road intersection on left. Begin climb.

11.7 Top of hill.

12.4 Interstate 280.

14.0 Santa Cruz Avenue intersection.

14.2 Right onto recreation path immediately after crossing San Franciaquito Creek bridge.

14.7 Left on Campus Drive West at stop sign.

16.0 Left on Galvez Street. End of ride.

■

a narrow, lush canyon with a canopy of bay laurel and sycamore trees along Corte Madera Creek. After several miles the pavement ends at a green gate. It's 2.5 miles to Page Mill Road on the dirt road.

Turn right onto Portola Road at the stop sign, where there's a convenience store, a gas station, and a small shopping center. Windy Hill is the bald grassy knoll you see to the west. Adventurous cyclists enjoy riding up and down Windy Hill from Skyline Boulevard on Spring Ridge Road, an old ranch road that joins Portola Valley Road just past the Sequoias retirement community. Windy Hill lies in a large open space preserve founded in 1987.

Portola Valley's town center is a mile and a half from Portola and Alpine roads. City council meetings are held in a school built directly on the San Andreas Fault, which formed the valley. (Perhaps that's why the town council is often split on important issues.) The town center has a small shopping center in a redwood grove across the street from the school, a nursery, three churches, and a walnut orchard.

Cable car inventor Andrew Hallidie lived in Portola Valley in the 1880s. He built an experimental tramway from the valley floor into the western foothills, which was located across the road from the shopping center.

As you leave town there's a gradual downhill. In a curve near the bottom of the hill you'll pass Old LaHonda Road (see LaHonda ride). Portola Road crosses a marshy inlet of Searsville reservoir. In the 1860s Searsville was located nearby. The town grew on the strength of the logging industry and a short-lived silver "strike." But in 1879 a federal court ordered the town's residents to relocate and make way for the reservoir, which was built in 1891, ostensibly to meet San Francisco's water needs, though it was never used for this purpose. Today it is the Jasper Ridge Biological Preserve owned by Stanford University.

You'll pass three more intersections—Portola Road "Cutoff," Manzanita Way, and Whiskey Hill Road—all on the left. The ride back to Interstate 280 on Sand Hill Road has a .7-mile climb, passing a large equestrian park on the left and a Christmas tree farm on the right. Stanford University's two-mile-long linear accelerator visible behind the tree farm looks like the world's longest two-car garage. Sand Hill Road, one of the oldest roads in San Mateo County, was used as early as the 1790s by Spanish settlers harvesting timber for the Bay Area's missions.

At the top of the climb on Sand Hill you'll have a grand view of the bay and East Bay mountains. Descend to Santa Cruz Avenue and continue straight. Cross San Francisquito Creek and immediately turn right on a bike path that takes you to Campus Drive West. Turn left and return to the stadium.

Distance: **28 miles.**
Terrain: **Rolling or flat.**
Traffic: **Light to moderate on Sundays.**

12. San Francisco

Mileage Log

0.0 Start mileage at Embarcadero and Folsom. There's plenty of free parking here. Ride north on Embarcadero.

0.3 Ferry Building on right.

1.7 Embarcadero becomes Jefferson Street.

1.8 Fisherman's Wharf.

2.2 Dolphin South End Club and Maritime Museum on right. Road becomes recreation path.

2.6 Left at Municipal Pier.

3.1 Right at Laguna, then left on Marina recreation path.

4.0 Enter U.S. Army gate to Presidio.

▼

San Francisco, a picturesque city with a fascinating history and marvelous architecture, also has its share of traffic congestion. Riding a bicycle may seem hazardous, but if you know when and where to ride, you can see the city at your leisure.

San Francisco has notoriously steep hills. They're mostly located downtown in cable car country. Riding around the city's perimeter next to the bay and ocean you can avoid the steepest hills, which even strong riders find daunting. Riding along the perimeter will also give you a view of some of the city's famous landmarks, including the Golden Gate Bridge, the Bay Bridge, Fisherman's Wharf, the Pacific Coast, and Golden Gate Park.

The San Francisco tour starts at the intersection of Folsom and Embarcadero next to San Francisco Bay. There's plenty of free parking on Sundays along Embarcadero. You'll ride north on the waterfront, south next to the Pacific, and then east through Golden Gate Park, looping back through the heart of the city. After your ride it's only a short walk to the Embarcadero Center, where you'll be dazzled by the spacious and striking Hyatt Regency hotel with its spaceship-like free-standing elevators.

Follow the city's piers north on the flat, wide Embarcadero. In 1987 a maze of railroad tracks was paved over, making cycling much safer here. As you pass the Embarcadero Center on your left you'll parallel elevated Highway 480. This freeway, which ends abruptly, was planned to continue

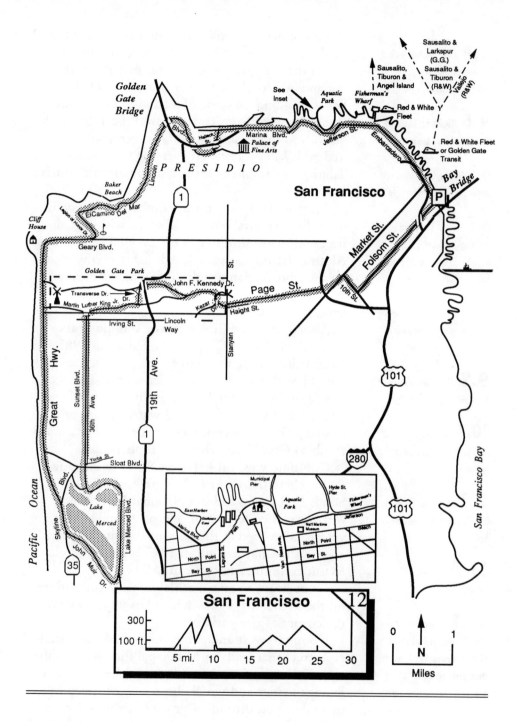

Golden
Gate
Bridge

See
Inset

Aquatic
Park

Fisherman's
Wharf

Sausalito &
Larkspur
(G.G.)

Sausalito,
Tiburon &
Angel Island

Sausalito &
Tiburon
(R&W)

Vallejo
(R&W)

Red & White
Fleet

Marina Blvd.

Palace of
Fine Arts

Jefferson St.

Embarcadero

Red & White Fleet
or Golden Gate
Transit

Halleck
St.

Lincoln

Blvd.

P R E S I D I O

San Francisco

Bay
Bridge

P

Baker
Beach

1

Legion of Honor Dr.

El Camino Del Mar

Market St.

Folsom St.

Cliff
House

Geary Blvd.

Golden   Gate   Park

St.

John F. Kennedy Dr.

Page   St.

10th St.

Transverse Dr.

Martin Luther King Jr. Dr.

Kezar

Haight St.

Dr.

Irving St.

Lincoln
Way

Stanyan

Great   Hwy.

Sunset Blvd.

36th   Ave.

19th   Ave.

101

1

280

Yorba St.

Sloat Blvd.

101

Pacific   Ocean

Blvd.

Lake
Merced

Lake Merced Blvd.

San Francisco Bay

Skyline

John Muir Dr.

35

Municipal
Pier

Hyde St.
Pier

Fisherman's
Wharf

East Harbor

Aquatic
Park

Gashouse
Cove

Marina Blvd.

Laguna St.

Nat'l Maritime
Museum

Jefferson

BEACH

Van Ness Ave.

North Point

North   Point

Bay   St.

Bay   St.

San Francisco

300

100 ft.

12

5 mi.   10   15   20   25   30

0   1

N

Miles

4.4 Left on Halleck Street under Hwy. 101 bridge at stop sign.

4.6 Right on Lincoln Boulevard at stop sign.

6.1 Golden Gate Bridge parking lot entrance on right .

6.7 Lincoln Boulevard summit. Begin descent. Lincoln becomes El Camino del Mar at bottom of hill.

8.7 Legion of Honor art museum on right. Keep left of Legion of Honor Drive.

9.2 Right on Geary Boulevard at stop sign.

10.2 Cliff House restaurant on right. Keep clear of parked cars.

11.3 Take Great Highway bike lane or recreation path on left.

13.3 San Francisco Zoo on left.

14.1 Right on Skyline Boulevard at stop sign or cross Skyline and pick up Lake Merced recreation path.

▼

along the bay and link with Highway 101, but a public outcry in the 1960s stopped it in mid-air.

On the right you'll see the historic Ferry Building and World Trade Center built in 1898. The Ferry Building was one of a handful of buildings along the waterfront that survived the 1906 earthquake and fire. The Golden Gate Ferry and the Red and White Fleet, with service to Sausalito, Tiburon, and Vallejo, serve commuters and tourists from here.

After another mile on the Embarcadero you'll reach Fisherman's Wharf at Pier 45 with its fishing fleet and many shops. You can take harbor cruises, Alcatraz Island tours, or watch fishermen working on their boats. Among the shops there's even a store that sells products made especially for left-handed people.

A section of the Embarcadero was along the route of the Coors Classic bicycle race in 1985. Competitors rode through a large warehouse on Pier 45 and along a narrow pier with a sharp corner. Skin divers were located in the bay to pluck errant cyclists out of the cold water in case of a mishap. The two-week race's prologue was a steep climb to Coit Tower from the Embarcadero.

Continue west on Jefferson Street to Aquatic Park, where there's a beach, a park, the Dolphin South End Club, and the National Maritime Museum. A collection of one-of-a-kind sailing vessels is moored at the museum. Tours are offered aboard the Thayer, built in 1895, and the Eureka, a Marin commuter ferry from 1890 to 1957.

If you want to take a cable car ride, you can get on the Hyde Street line, which has its terminus at the corner of the park.

Continue west and climb a short hill to a dead-end street that leads to Municipal Pier. Ride to the end of the pier for a better view of the bay. Turn left at the pier and you'll climb a short, steep hill that takes you through a grove of cypress located at Fort Mason. On your right you'll see the *Jeremiah O'Brien* merchant ship, one of hundreds built in

The Palace of Fine Arts was built in 1915 for the Panama-Pacific International Expo commemorating completion of the Panama Canal.

San Francisco harbor to transport military goods during World War II. It's now a floating museum.

The San Francisco International Youth Hostel is located in Fort Mason. Call (415) 863-1444 for more information about overnight housing at low cost. Reservations are required at this popular hostel.

You'll ride a short distance on a dirt path in an open grassy area before returning to pavement at Laguna Street and Marina Boulevard. You can ride on Marina or take a paved recreation path to your right, beyond the parking lot. Along the bay you'll see the Marina Green and the Marina small craft harbor.

At the end of Marina Green walk your bike across Marina Boulevard to visit the red sandstone-like Roman columns of the Palace of Fine Arts, which was built in 1915 for the Panama-Pacific Exposition. Bicycles are not allowed on the

14.6 Left on John Muir Drive at traffic light.

15.7 Left on Lake Merced Boulevard at stop sign.

17.7 Keep right at junction. Lake Merced Boulevard becomes Sunset Boulevard, and you can take Sunset all the way to Golden Gate Park. Traffic is heavy on Sunset after 9 a.m.; 36th Street, which parallels Sunset, is an alternative. Reach it as follows:

▼

18.0 Ride under Sloat Avenue and turn right on Yorba Street.

18.1 Left on 36th Street.

20.0 Left on Irving Street at stop sign and then immediately turn right on Sunset Boulevard at traffic light. Ride under Lincoln Way overpass.

20.2 Right on Martin Luther King Junior Drive at stop sign.

20.8 Mallard Lake on right. Giant ferns on right at mile 20.9.

21.2 Left on Transverse Drive. A difficult turn to make when traffic is heavy.

21.4 Keep right at junction with West Drive.

21.6 Right on Kennedy Drive at stop sign. Road closed to auto traffic every Sunday.

22.5 DeYoung Museum on right.

▼

grounds, but you can park your bike and take a stroll on a path around the lagoon with its many waterfowl. The Exploratorium, a hands-on science museum, is also located here. For more information about the Exploratorium call (415) 563-3200.

Return to Marina Boulevard and ride through the Presidio, headquarters for the Sixth Army. The base is open to the public on weekends. One of the original adobe buildings built by the first Spanish settlers in 1776 is located on the base near the intersection of Arguello Boulevard and Funston Avenue. The army museum is located on Funston Avenue at Lincoln Boulevard. For more information call (415) 561-4115.

As you ride through the base and climb steadily on Lincoln Boulevard you'll be surrounded by tall cypress and eucalyptus. Before riding under Highway 101 turn into the parking lot on your right for views of the Golden Gate Bridge.

Shortly past the Highway 101 overpass you'll begin a long descent on Lincoln, which becomes El Camino del Mar. You'll see some beautiful Mediterranean-style houses, with spectacular views of the Golden Gate Bridge and the Marin Headlands.

You'll leave the houses as you climb past the Lincoln Park Golf Course and Lincoln Park. Turn left at the Palace of the Legion of Honor art museum (415) 750-3600 , which displays a large collection of prints and drawings of the American West. The World War I memorial is patterned after the Palace of the Legion of Honor in Paris.

Now it's downhill to Geary Boulevard, followed by a steep downhill to the Great Highway and The Esplanade along the Pacific Ocean. Ride in the outer lane as you pass the Cliff House Restaurant to avoid cars backing out from parking spaces. The Cliff House was built in a dramatic setting overlooking Seal Rock in 1858 by Sam Brannan. It was originally assembled from lumber salvaged off a wrecked schooner, but has burned and been rebuilt several times. Geary Boulevard becomes the Great Highway along the coast. Don't miss the Dutch windmills on your left in Golden Gate Park. A volunteer organization restored one of the windmills to its former glory.

A recreation path completed in 1988 can be ridden on the left side of the Great Highway, or you can ride along the highway's wide shoulder. The San Francisco Zoo is located on Sloat Boulevard near the Great Highway. Continue south on the Great Highway up a short hill and descend to Skyline Boulevard. Cross the road and pick up the recreation path along Lake Merced or turn right and then turn left onto John Muir Drive.

Lake Merced Boulevard has a narrow recreation path with lots of pedestrian traffic. Continue north on Sunset Boulevard, ride under the Sloat Boulevard overpass, and then turn right on Yorba Street. Take an immediate left and ride to Golden Gate Park on 36th Avenue.

Golden Gate Park extends three miles inland from the ocean. John McLaren, a Scottish landscape gardener and park superintendent from 1887 to 1943, turned sand dunes and scrub into the green paradise that the park is today. There's a gradual mile climb to Transverse Drive. Kennedy Drive is closed to car traffic on Sundays from 6 a.m. to 5 p.m.

On Kennedy you'll see the de Young Museum on the right and the beautiful white-glass Conservatory of Flowers on the left near the end of the street. California millionaire James Lick had the entire building packed in London and shipped around the Horn.

After riding under the Kezar Drive walkway, you'll cross Stanyan Street at a crosswalk and pick up Page Street one block to the north. Stanyan Street Cyclery is located at 672 Stanyan between Haight and Page (415) 221-7211 . You'll get a sample of the city's famous Victorian-style houses on Page. Although Page has many stop signs, traf-

22.8 Conservatory of Flowers on left.

22.9 Right on paved path (note green bike route sign) that parallels Kezar Drive.

23.1 Go right down hill, turn left and ride through tunnel under Kezar.

23.2 Path ends at crosswalk signal at Haight and Stanyan. Turn left here onto Stanyan. Stanyan Cyclery on right.

23.3 Right on Page Street.

25.1 Market Street left merge at traffic light.

25.3 Right on Tenth Street at traffic light.

25.7 Left on Folsom Avenue at traffic light.

27.5 Return to start.
■

fic is light and the hills are manageable. It's mostly downhill to Market Street, the main street through downtown San Francisco. Ride on Market three blocks, turn right onto 10th Street (one way) and then left on Folsom. This straight, wide one-way street returns you to the Embarcadero. Downtown traffic is light on Sundays.

13. Tunitas Creek Road

Distance: **37 miles.**
Terrain: **Hilly.**
Traffic: **Light to moderate.**

San Mateo County has many roads winding through the redwoods that seem to be made for bicycling, especially Tunitas Creek Road and Kings Mountain Road. On this tour of mountain and ocean you'll leave Woodside and have two long climbs and descents.

Woodside School on Highway 84 is a good place to start. Next to the school there's a small white building called Independence Hall, which served as a school in its early years and has been moved three times.

Riding on Albion Avenue, a residential street, you'll pass wooded estates, but don't miss the old-fashioned log cabin on the right. Blackberries flourishing on the roadside make a tasty treat in the summer. On Kings Mountain Road you'll see Woodside Store museum on the left just as the climb begins. Restored in the early 1980s, it's the town's oldest building (built in 1854). Tripp Road, where the store stands, is named for store owner Robert Tripp. The well-known figure was a dentist, saloon keeper, postmaster, and one of the original county supervisors. His store did a thriving trade with loggers and teamsters hauling redwood logs to the port of Redwood City.

Kings Mountain Road climbs to Skyline Boulevard through redwoods, oaks, bay laurels, and tan oaks. The first .2 miles and a section about a mile from the top are the steepest. Many road signs around these parts have bullet holes, put there by our best marksmen. But not the Huddart Park

Mileage Log

0.0 Start mileage at Woodside Town Hall and school on Highway 84, .2 miles west of the Cañada Road intersection. Ride west on Highway 84.

0.1 Right on Albion Avenue.

0.3 Left on Manuella Avenue.

0.9 Right on Kings Mountain Road at stop sign.

1.3 Woodside Store on left at Tripp Road. Keep right at next junction.

2.8 Huddart Park entrance.

4.1 Road widens briefly.
▼

5.3 Summit Springs Hotel site on right.

5.7 Skyline Boulevard junction at stop sign. Cross road to Tunitas Creek Road.

6.9 Star Hill Road on left.

7.9 Trailhead to Purisima Creek Road on right.

8.7 Shingle Mill Road on left. Private property.

10.4 Mitchell Creek Road on left. Private property.

11.3 Lobitos Creek Road on right. Dirt road to Highway 1.

13.0 Lobitos Creek Cutoff on right. Paved road to Highway 1. Keep left on Tunitas Creek Road.

15.0 Left on Highway 1 at stop sign.

16.0 Old entrance to Star Hill Road on left.

16.6 Left on Stage Road.

17.7 Left on Highway 84 at stop sign. Peterson and Alsford General Merchandise store on corner.

▼

sign. Its big, bold, yellow letters are made of thick steel plate.

Midway up the narrow road you'll notice a wide section. In the mid-1960s a wooden bridge needed replacement, so the county went to great expense to remove it and widen the road in more than Oriental splendor. The locals, however, did not appreciate having their country road turned into a freeway. Coincidentally, other parts of Kings Mountain Road subsequently went with little repair for the next 10 years.

Near Skyline Boulevard on your right you'll pass a meadow, site of the infamous Summit Springs Hotel, where mountain men met mountain women for friendly games of checkers.

Tunitas Creek Road begins at the summit and goes to the coast. It was called Froment's Road when built in 1868 by Eugene Froment, who used it to haul logs from his sawmill at the Lobitos Creek Cutoff junction on Tunitas Creek. It was a toll road until the county bought it in 1884 for $3,000, paving it in 1936.

There's a gradual descent for two miles followed by steep hairpin curves that are often wet in the winter and on foggy mornings. The narrow, jolting road follows Tunitas Creek to the ocean. Some of the old logging roads nearby include Purisima Creek, Star Hill, Swett, Richards, Shingle Mill, and Lobitos Creek. Star Hill is another toll road that went to the coast, but it was abandoned after San Mateo County bought it.

Open-space land north of Tunitas Creek can be reached by taking the old logging road on the right (described in Mileage Log) that joins Purisima Creek Road; there's another rugged trail going over Bald Knob to Irish Ridge Road. Some of these roads cross private property.

Where Tunitas Creek Road joins Highway 1 you'll see flower farms. Turn left, immediately cross Tunitas Creek, and begin a half-mile climb. Highway 1 has a wide shoulder most of the way to Stage Road, which is at the top of the hill.

Turn left on Stage Road and ride down to San Gregorio, where there is food and drink. Continue up Highway 84 to Skyline Boulevard. It's a gradual climb, with the steepest part coming a couple miles above LaHonda. At the summit village of Sky Londa you'll begin a descent on Highway 84 to Woodside. Watch out for the first few curves; they're often wet and oily. At the bottom continue straight and it's only a couple of miles into town under the shade of giant eucalyptus trees.

19.8 Bear Gulch Road on left.

24.8 Ken Kesey house on right.

25.8 Pioneer Market in LaHonda on left.

29.1 Old LaHonda Road on right.

31.9 Skyline Boulevard.

35.3 Portola Road on right.

35.7 Wunderlich Park on left.

36.4 Tripp Road on left.

37.4 End of ride at Woodside School on right.

■

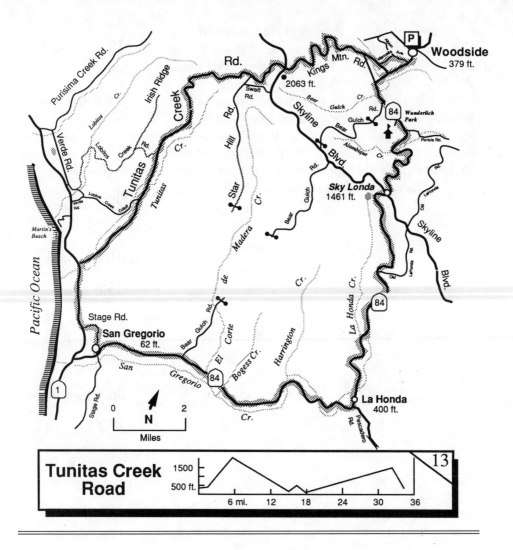

Tunitas Creek Road

1500
500 ft.

6 mi.　12　18　24　30　36

13

14. Berkeley-Oakland Hills

Distance: **28 miles.**
Terrain: **Hilly.**
Traffic: **Light to moderate.**

You'll find spectacular views of the bay, its bridges, and San Francisco from Skyline Boulevard on the crest of the East Bay hills. Getting there by bike is half the fun. The ups and downs in this ride take you through redwood forests, rural communities, and numerous regional parks offering a variety of activities.

This tour begins at Inspiration Point in Tilden Regional Park, on a hilltop overlooking San Pablo Reservoir. Go left from the parking lot on Wildcat Canyon Road, where you'll begin a long descent on the bumpy two-lane road. Turn right at the bottom of the hill on Camino Pablo, which runs the length of Moraga Valley and has a wide shoulder.

The first town you'll pass is Orinda, at the intersection of Camino Pablo and Highway 24, formerly called The Crossroads. Ranchers settled here in the 1870s. The California and Nevada Railroad linked Orinda to Berkeley in 1890, bringing further growth. In 1903 a road tunnel was built through the East Bay hills just south of the Caldecott Tunnel. The old tunnel was closed with the completion of Caldecott in 1937.

There's a gentle climb and descent through rural countryside to Moraga. Joaquin Moraga was one of the valley's first settlers in 1835, having received a land grant from the Mexican government. Moraga Way between Moraga and Orinda was built in 1889 in anticipation of the arrival of the California and Nevada railroad—which never made it. Con-

Mileage Log

0.0 Start mileage at Inspiration Point in Tilden Park at the summit of Wildcat Canyon Road. No services here. Turn left from parking lot and begin descent.

2.4 Right on Camino Pablo Road at stop sign.

4.5 Ride under Highway 24 overpass. Camino Pablo becomes Moraga Way.

4.6 Downtown Orinda on left at Brookwood Road.

9.2 Downtown Moraga. Right on Canyon Road at traffic light.

11.0 Left at Pinehurst Road junction and stop sign. Right goes steeply uphill to Skyline Boulevard. Begin climb.

12.2 Alameda County line. Sprint!

▼

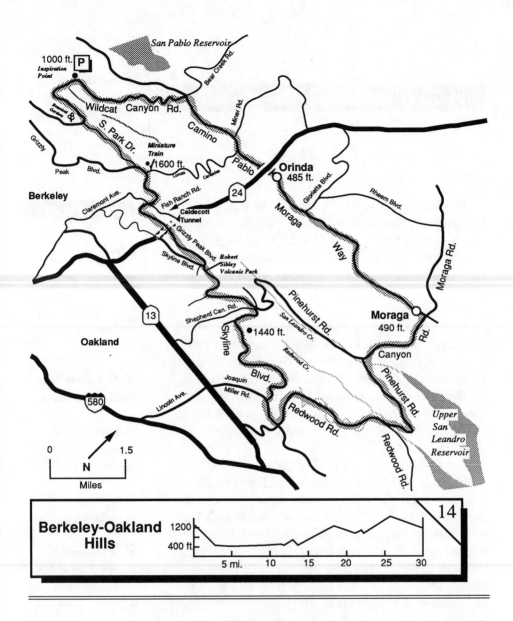

Berkeley-Oakland Hills 14

12.5 Summit. Begin 1.2-mile descent.

13.7 Right on Redwood Road at stop sign. Begin 4-mile climb.

▼

tinue on Moraga Way until the traffic light and turn right onto lightly traveled Canyon Road. The Moraga shopping center on the right was started by land developer Donald Rheem in 1950, replacing a pear orchard.

After a climb through grassy hillsides and a

grove of eucalyptus you'll descend to Pinehurst Road for a cool ride through the redwoods. The oldest and largest redwoods were logged from 1840 to '60. You can shorten the ride by about five miles if you go right. Pinehurst takes you to Skyline Boulevard through the "village" of Canyon, a former logging camp.

Turn left on Pinehurst for an easier ascent and a view of Upper San Leandro Reservoir, built in 1926 with a capacity of 13.5 billion gallons. In a couple of miles you'll reach Redwood Road, where you'll turn right. Food and drink are available at Redwood Lodge, a rustic store about a mile up Redwood Road. The climb continues past Skyline Boulevard at a shopping center as you turn right onto Joaquin Miller Road before taking another right onto Skyline Boulevard. The East Bay Regional Parks administration building is on Miller Road.

Skyline rolls along the ridge of the East Bay hills through residential areas and eucalyptus groves, offering some of the best panoramas of San Francisco and the Golden Gate Bridge. After passing Robert Sibley Volcanic Park on your right, there's a key right turn without a stop sign that you'll take to pick up Grizzly Peak Boulevard. After a short descent you'll come to the Fish Ranch Road intersection. Continue straight, uphill. After some more climbing you'll reach a park with a miniature steam train. The train runs from 11 a.m. to 6 p.m. on weekends all year, and from 1 p.m. to 6 p.m. on weekdays during school spring and summer vacations.

A quarter-mile past the train turn right onto South Park Drive for a straight descent. Watch for cars leaving parking lots on both sides of the road. Follow South Park to Wildcat Canyon and take it back to Inspiration Point. At Wildcat and South Park you can visit the botanical gardens for a sample of California's diverse plant life; they're open from 10 a.m. to 5 p.m. You'll find almost every plant native to the state included in the 6.6-acre

16.1 Right on Joaquin Miller Road at stop sign.

16.7 Right at Skyline Boulevard junction.

17.7 Summit.

19.4 Keep right at junction with Carlsbrook Drive.

19.8 Water fountain on right at parking lot for Skyline Gate staging area in Redwood Regional Park.

20.2 Pinehurst Road junction. Shallow left. Skyline continues level.

20.8 Keep right at Snake Road junction. Begin 1.3-mile climb.

21.7 Water fountain on right at Robert Sibley Park entrance.

21.8 Right on Grizzly Peak Road.

22.1 Summit. Road levels. Crossing Caldecott Tunnel.

22.4 View of Bay Area on left; 23.5 view.

24.0 Begin .2-mile descent.

▼

Tilden Park's miniature train attracts riders young and old.

24.2 Straight on Grizzly Peak Road at 4-way stop. Begin 1.4-mile climb.

25.4 Steam train park on right. Water fountain at entrance.

25.6 Right on South Park Drive, crossing train tunnel. Begin 1.5-mile descent.

27.1 Right on Wildcat Canyon Road at stop sign. Botanical Gardens straight ahead. Begin 1.2-mile climb.

28.3 End of ride at Inspiration Point.

garden that has been divided into sections: Southern California, Shasta-Cascade, Valley, Santa Lucia, Channel Islands, Sierran, Redwood, Sea Bluff, Pacific Rain Forest, Franciscan, Antioch Dunes, Coastal Dunes, and Pond. A pond, sand dunes, and Wildcat Creek add to the garden's beauty.

Celebrate the finish with a picnic at Inspiration Point. From the parking lot walk or ride north on Nimitz Way, a good place to see the sun set behind the Golden Gate Bridge. The paved recreation path, formerly a service road to Nike missile sites, extends north along the ridge for four miles.

15. Calaveras Road

Distance: **37 miles.**
Terrain: **One long hill, otherwise flat.**
Traffic: **Moderate.**

Few locations in the East Bay can match Calaveras Road for its remote setting and endless succession of twists and turns through wooded hillsides. Tucked away at the entrance to Sunol Valley, the road passes through the San Francisco Water Department/Hetch Hetchy watershed. Traffic is always light, and on Sunday mornings you may see only one or two cars, not to mention a hairy tarantula crawling across the road. Besides the blue expanse of Calaveras Reservoir, you'll see the rocky bluff of Apperson Ridge towering over the dam, a favorite destination for hikers in Sunol Regional Wilderness.

This ride starts from the Vallejo Mill Historical Park at the entrance to Niles Canyon in Fremont. A waterwheel-powered flour mill that used grinding stones imported from France was operated here by Don Jose de Jesus Vallejo from 1853 until 1884. Picnic tables are now located on the site, which is marked by a plaque.

The ride through Niles Canyon follows Alameda Creek on a gentle grade to Sunol. Along the way you'll see railroad tracks on both sides of the canyon: the defunct Southern Pacific line on the north and the active Union Pacific line on the south. The transcontinental railroad was built through the canyon in 1862, and the road was completed seven years later. Highway 84 is a two-lane road with a fair amount of traffic most of the day.

If you want to ride through downtown Sunol,

Mileage Log

0.0 Start mileage at roadside picnic area at northeast corner of Highway 84 and Mission Boulevard. Ride east on Niles Canyon Road, Highway 84.

1.1 Railroad bridge over highway and Alameda Creek.

2.4 Narrow bridge.

3.0 Train tunnel.

3.4 Narrow bridge. Train tunnel on right.

5.9 Exit right into town of Sunol. Grocery store, post office, and gas station.

6.2 Continue east through downtown Sunol.

▼

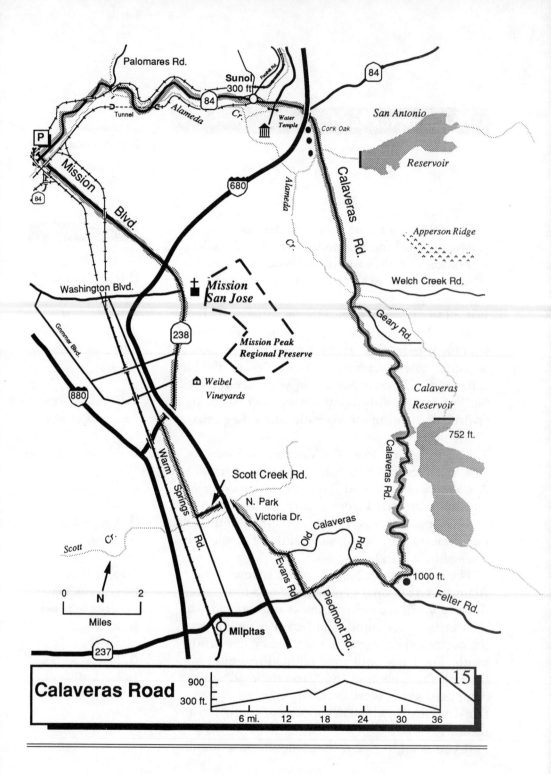

Palomares Rd.

Sunol
300 ft.

Tunnel

Alameda Cr.

P

Mission Blvd.

680

84

Water Temple

Cork Oak

San Antonio

Reservoir

Alameda Cr.

Calaveras Rd.

Apperson Ridge

Welch Creek Rd.

Washington Blvd.

✝ **Mission San Jose**

238

Mission Peak Regional Preserve

Geary Rd.

Grimmer Blvd.

880

⌂ **Weibel Vineyards**

Warm Springs Rd.

Calaveras Reservoir

752 ft.

Calaveras Rd.

Scott Creek Rd.

N. Park
Victoria Dr.

Scott Cr.

Old Calaveras Rd.

Evans Rd.

Piedmont Rd.

1000 ft.

Felter Rd.

0   **N**   2
Miles

○ **Milpitas**

237

Calaveras Road

900
300 ft.

6 mi.   12   18   24   30   36

15

turn right and exit Highway 84 before the train subway. There's a store in town that sells sandwiches, food, and drink. Ride through town and turn left at the next stop sign to return to Highway 84.

The Hetch Hetchy pipeline passes a short distance south of Sunol. A monument to the vital aqueduct is located at the junction of Highway 84 and Pleasanton-Sunol Road: Look for the impressive Roman columns on the right in an onion field. A similar monument is located north of Woodside on Cañada Road.

Calaveras Road begins at the stop sign shortly after you ride under Interstate 680. Cork oak trees line the road on the right. However, the Bay Area climate is too wet for the bark to grow thick enough for harvesting. As you cross Alameda Creek the road begins climbing. Among the birds you'll see near the creek in the spring are woodpeckers, red-wing blackbirds, red-tail hawks, cliff swallows, magpies, scrub jays, kingfishers, and warblers. Turkey vultures (and sometimes eagles) soar above Calaveras Road on thermal updrafts.

Calaveras Reservoir, completed in 1925, was built by Spring Valley Water Works. The reservoir, with depths reaching 150 feet, holds 31.5 billion gallons of water, the largest storage capacity in the Bay Area. Spring Valley was purchased by the San Francisco Water Department shortly after the dam's completion. A pipeline under the bay connecting the Alameda Creek reservoir system with San Francisco dates back to 1888.

You'll pass numerous small creeks that flow into the reservoir year round. Sometimes these creeks overflow and destroy portions of the road. At the summit you'll have a sweeping view of the valley and San Jose to the southwest.

The character of the ride changes from rural expanses to urban hustle and bustle in Milpitas and north to Fremont. However, Evans Road and North Park Victoria Drive are lightly traveled frontage roads at the base of the foothills. On Scott

6.3 Left to return to Highway 84 at stop sign.

6.4 Right at stop sign. Hetch Hetchy water temple is open weekdays, 7:30 a.m. to 4:30 p.m. Enter at an onion field just beyond the intersection on right.

7.2 Ride under Interstate 680. Calaveras Road begins.

7.4 Cork oak trees on right.

11.1 Alameda Creek. Begin climb.

14.0 False summit and meadow.

20.9 Summit. Begin steep descent.

21.2 Right on Felter Road at stop sign.

22.1 Ed Levin County Park. Drinking fountains and restrooms.

23.6 Right on Evans Road. Name changes to North Park Victoria Boulevard at 24.9 miles.

▼

26.4 Left on Scott Creek Road at stop sign. Ride under Interstate 680 at 26.5 miles.

27.0 Right on Warm Springs Boulevard at traffic light.

29.0 Right on Mission Boulevard at traffic light. Interstate 680 at 29.6 miles.

30.0 Weibel Vineyards and Mission Peak Regional Preserve entrance on right.

32.3 Mission San Jose de Guadalupe on right. Food stores, gas stations, and restaurants nearby.

36.5 Right on Highway 84 at traffic light.

36.6 Left at roadside parking area. End of ride.

■

Creek Road there's an old farm house that seems out of place next to Interstate 680 and modern houses.

Warm Springs Boulevard is a four-lane divided road with bike lanes. Be careful riding on Mission Boulevard, where you'll find a large shopping center and ramps for Interstate 680. North of Interstate 680, Mission Boulevard becomes two lanes with a wide shoulder. Weibel Winery and Mission Peak Regional Preserve are on the right off Mission Boulevard. However, the vineyards are slated for removal to make room for housing.

When the Spaniards settled here they built a series of missions from San Francisco to Santa Barbara. Mission San Jose de Guadalupe on Mission Boulevard consists of a white adobe mission and church among oaks and tall palm trees lining the road. The mission was founded in 1797 by Francisco de Lausen. Indians who lived here frequently revolted and were subdued by Spanish soldiers. One revolt in 1830 was put down by none other than Kit Carson. Carson was preceded at the mission by another great Western explorer and fur trapper, Jedediah Smith, in 1827. The mission museum is open daily from 10 a.m. to 4 p.m.

16. Clayton

Distance: **51 miles.**
Terrain: **Hilly.**
Traffic: **Heavy in Walnut Creek, light elsewhere.**

There's a road in Contra Costa County that's so remote, even bicyclists who live nearby don't know about it. The narrow, winding Morgan Territory Road is also one of the most scenic in the Bay Area. It's a perfect place to escape from the busy San Ramon Valley.

This tour starts in Danville and circles the base of Mt. Diablo. As you leave from Railroad Avenue next to California Pedaler bike shop you'll see the old Southern Pacific train depot built at the turn of the century. The train ride from here to San Francisco took two-and-a-half hours.

Danville remained a small farming town until the 1950s, when improved water service fostered rapid growth. Front Street, just east of Hartz Avenue, is the historic center of town along San Ramon Creek. Danville was named for the first settlers to the area in 1852, brothers Daniel and Andrew Inman.

Ride north on Hartz Avenue through downtown, which has the charm of Carmel without the crowds. As you ride to Walnut Creek you'll pass ranches and acres of walnut orchards planted at the turn of the century. It's a pleasant ride in early spring when yellow mustard carpets the orchards. Wheat was grown here in the late 1880s, later replaced by vineyards and fruit orchards.

Riding through Walnut Creek can be hectic in traffic, so get an early start. Main Street and its older buildings seem lost among the larger modern structures of this contemporary city. Walnut Creek

Mileage Log

0.0 Start mileage at the intersection of Church Street and Railroad Avenue next to California Pedaler bike shop at 295 S. Hartz Avenue (415) 820-0345. Ride north on Hartz Avenue, which becomes Danville Boulevard.

5.0 Walnut Creek city limits sign. Sprint!

5.5 Interstate 680 overpass. Danville becomes S. California Boulevard then N. California Boulevard.

6.7 **Right on Civic Drive at traffic light. Becomes Oak Road.**

8.1 **Right on Contra Costa Canal recreation trail. Watch for the yellow "trail crossing" sign.**

▼

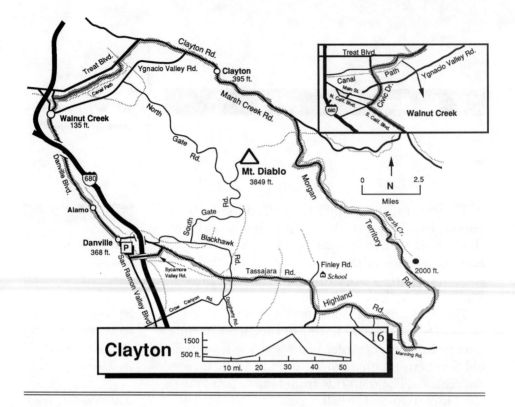

Clayton

1500
500 ft.

10 mi. 20 30 40 50

16

11.2 Left at junction over bridge.

11.6 Right on Treat Boulevard.

13.4 Right on Clayton Road at traffic light.

17.1 Downtown Clayton.

19.5 Rodie's Store on left. Last chance for food or drink until Danville.

▼

has changed dramatically in the past quarter-century. Located on the historic east–west wagon road and stagecoach route from Martinez to San Jose, the town was no more than a few houses and stores in its early days. The valley remained a quiet rural setting until shortly after World War II.

For a few miles you'll ride on Contra Costa Canal recreation path, one of the most popular recreation routes in Contra Costa County. Watch for pedestrians and other cyclists. Use caution crossing streets. You'll leave the canal at Treat Boulevard and ride south on Clayton Road, a wide, busy commercial road. But visiting Clayton is like taking a step back in time. The town resembles a movie set, with many buildings from the late 1880s. Clayton was established in 1857 by Joel Clayton, a San Francisco dairyman. Coal and copper mines in the nearby hills kept the town alive.

Morgan Territory Road rises 2,000 feet to a spectacular overlook of San Ramon Valley.

In the late 1800s vineyards were planted and wineries sprang up. Today residential subdivisions nearly surround this historic town.

Leaving Clayton you'll have an impressive view

21.4 Right on Morgan Territory Road. In 4 miles road narrows.

▼

Ranch land on Highland Road is fast giving way to development.

30.6 Morgan Territory Regional Preserve parking area on left. Toilets, hiking, off-road riding available.

31.0 Summit. Begin descent to Manning Road.

36.0 Right on Manning Road at stop sign.

36.9 Right on Highland Road at stop sign. Alameda-Contra Costa county line sign at 37.0. Sprint!

41.6 Right on Tassajara Road at stop sign.

▼

of the eastern face of Mt. Diablo with its steep, rocky slope. A couple of miles from Clayton you'll enter a long, wide valley leading to Morgan Territory Road.

Legend has it that Jeremiah Morgan discovered this rugged area in 1856 while hunting on Mt. Diablo. As he looked out over the hills he declared all the land within view to be his, about 10,000 acres worth.

At the junction with Morgan Territory Road there's a small housing development, but the narrow valley soon changes to open countryside. Before you know it you're in a narrow canyon under a canopy of oak trees following Marsh Creek. The climb takes you steadily to 2,000 feet. At the summit you're rewarded with a view of farm and ranch lands to the west and south. A brisk descent takes you to Manning Road, where it's a flat ride back to Danville. Along the way you'll pass numerous old farms. Be sure to stop and see Tassajara School on Finley Road. It's a classic one-room school built in 1888, surrounded by

A classic one-room schoolhouse can be found on Finley Road.

42.8 Finley Road on right. Old Tassajara School about a mile up road on right.

49.0 Keep left on Sycamore Valley Road.

50.4 Interstate 680 overpass.

50.6 Right on San Ramon Valley Boulevard at traffic light, which becomes S. Hartz Avenue.

51.2 End ride at Church Street and Railroad Avenue off South Hartz Avenue.

■

stately old walnut trees and with a bell tower and turnstile out front.

As you head back to Danville on Tassajara Road you'll pass "executive homes" in the Blackhawk development. Residents spare no expense at making themselves visibly comfortable. For example, one house is touted to have 13 color televisions, a baby grand piano, a swimming pool, and enough remote controls for stereos and VCRs to supply a small country. The Blackhawk developer lives in a 30,000-square-foot residence with wall-to-wall sound that includes 105 stereo speakers throughout the house.

17. Mount Diablo State Park

Distance: **29 miles.**
Terrain: **Mountainous.**
Traffic: **Light to moderate.**

The first question people ask about Mt. Diablo is whether it's a volcano. The answer is no. The second question is why would anybody want to ride a bike to the mountain's 3,849-foot summit? You'll learn the answer on top. One-third of the state can be seen from the summit on a clear day.

Bicyclists have been riding up the mountain ever since a toll road was built in 1879 at a cost of $12,000. A group of businessmen calling themselves the Mt. Diablo Summit Road Company planned to draw tourists to a 16-room hotel at the 2,500-foot level (three miles from the summit) and offer trips to the summit. The hotel was built shortly before the road's completion, drawing visitors from around the world. It was owned by R. N. Burgess, who had previously owned a hotel on Mt. Washington in New Hampshire.

In 1891 disaster struck and the summit observation platform burned down, with the hotel suffering the same fate soon afterwards. The toll road was closed and didn't reopen until 1915. In 1921 a parcel of land on Mt. Diablo was designated a state park, and over the years the park has grown to its present size.

This ride starts from downtown Danville and takes the south summit road, which meets the park's northern road at a ranger station 4.6 miles from the summit. You'll begin climbing as you ride east under Interstate 680, passing the Diablo Country Club on the left and Green Creek on the right. The south park entrance has two small stone

Mileage Log

0.0 Start mileage in Danville at corner of Church Street and Railroad Avenue next to California Pedaler bike shop at 295 S. Hartz Avenue (415) 820-0345. Ride north on Hartz Avenue.

0.2 Right on Diablo Road at traffic light.

0.5 Interstate 680 underpass.

0.8 Straight on Diablo Road at intersection with Camino Tassajara Road.

1.3 Right at stop sign, continuing on Diablo Road.

1.9 Continue straight at junction with Green Valley Road. Diablo Road name changes to Blackhawk Road.

▼

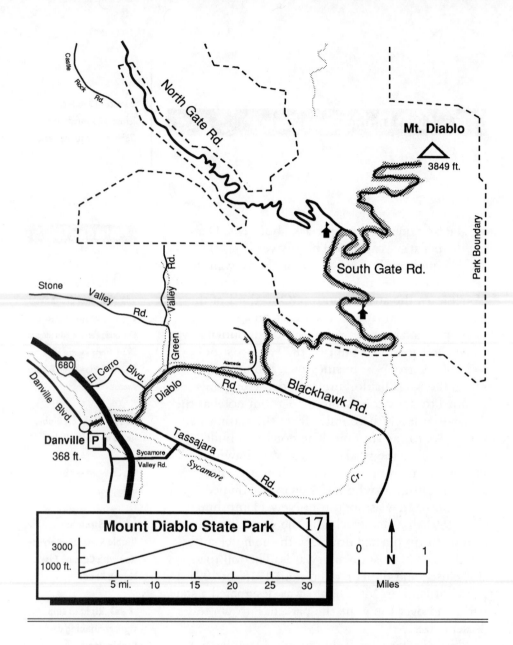

Mt. Diablo
3849 ft.

North Gate Rd.

Castle Rock Rd.

Park Boundary

South Gate Rd.

Stone Valley Rd.

Valley Rd.

Green Valley Rd.

680

El Cerro Blvd.

Diablo Rd.

Alameda

Diablo Rd.

Blackhawk Rd.

Danville Blvd.

Danville P
368 ft.

Tassajara

Sycamore Valley Rd.

Sycamore Rd.

Cr.

| Mount Diablo State Park | 17 |

3000
1000 ft.

5 mi.   10   15   20   25   30

0   N   1

Miles

3.4 Left on Mt. Diablo Scenic Boulevard. Look for green sign and two stone columns. Name changes to South Gate Road.

▼

columns and a weathered sign. The road hugs the side of the mountain as it winds upward at a steady grade of about 6 percent. In the spring the pleasant aroma of buckbrush (a member of the lilac family) permeates the fresh, cool air.

Cruising restrictions do not apply to bicycles. Mt. Diablo is in the background.

A massive rock outcropping can be found halfway up Mt. Diablo.

Maps of the park are available at the gate for 50 cents. Bicyclists pay no entry fee.

Near the ranger station you'll see a rock outcropping called Fossil Ridge, composed of sedimentary rocks. It was pushed up with the rest of the mountain millions of years ago. Fossils of sea life as well as of mastadons, sabretooth cats, and three-toed horses have been found here.

By this point on a warm day you'll be interested in finding water. Water fountains are located at the south ranger station and the main park office at the junction, another two miles up the road. Restrooms are to be found at many camp sites along the road. There's a drinking fountain and a restroom at the summit, but the food stand inside the rock building shut down long ago.

Turn right at the ranger station junction. The gradient steepens from here on. The mountain's south face features views of Livermore Valley and the Mt. Hamilton range. Near the summit there's a large parking area on the right and then a divided one-way road. Take the narrow road on the right, which has about an 18 percent grade for the next 300 yards. Walk up the rock tower for a view of the Sierra (on a clear day) to the east, Mt. Lassen to the north, Mt. Hamilton to the south, and the Farallon Islands to the west. Once you've caught your breath ride down the mountain, staying right on the one-way road. Turn left at the junction and head back through the south gate entrance, retracing your route to the bike shop.

7.4 South Gate park entrance.

9.7 Right on Summit Road at ranger station.

14.3 Summit. Return same route.

28.6 End of ride.
■

18. Orinda

0.0 Start mileage in downtown Orinda at intersection of Brookwood Road and Camino Pablo. Ride north on Camino Pablo.

0.2 Ride under Highway 24.

2.3 Bear Creek Road junction. Continue straight on San Pablo Dam Road.

7.7 **Right on Castro Ranch Road.**

10.0 **Right on Alhambra Valley Road.**

12.7 **Right on Bear Creek Road.**

14.2 Begin steep .6-mile climb.

16.9 Entrance to Briones Park on left.

▼

On this ride through the East Bay watershed you'll see sprawling ranches and the San Pablo Reservoir. Originally these rolling hills were part of the huge "Rancho El Sobrante" Mexican land grant purchased by Victor and Juan Castro in 1841. *Sobrante* is Spanish for "vacant" or "remaining." Squatters quickly moved in, and before long the land was parceled out. A son of one of the Castros built a ranch at the intersection of Castro Ranch Road and San Pablo Dam Road in 1868.

The ride starts in downtown Orinda, loops through Alhambra Valley, up Happy Valley Road, and back to town. As you pass under the busy Highway 24 overpass, imagine what life was like here in 1941 when this intersection had the distinction of acquiring the first traffic light in San Ramon Valley. San Pablo Dam Road was a dirt road until 1919; in 1952 it was widened and straightened to its present alignment. The first evidence of a building boom in the valley appears on Castro Ranch Road, where subdivisions are being built near the top of the short climb. However, in Alhambra Valley you'll enjoy a ride in the country with little traffic as you pass ranches and hay fields.

A challenging climb greets you on Bear Creek Road. It can be unpleasantly hot on summer days, so plan your ride accordingly. Bear Creek Road rolls up and down on the way to Happy Valley Road. Turn left and begin a one-mile ascent through evergreens and redwoods. Higher up

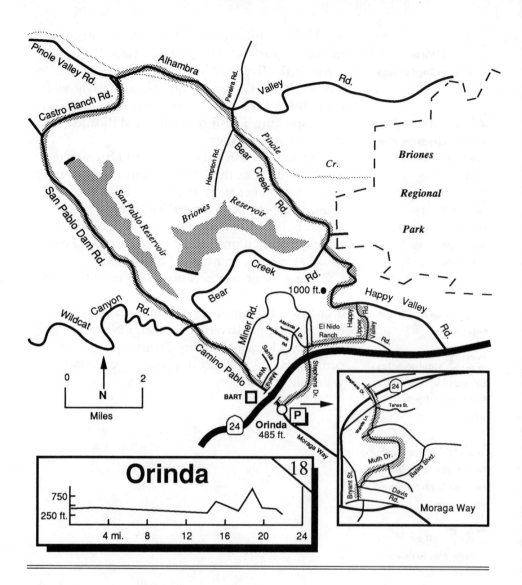

you'll pass new, exclusive houses before descending into Happy Valley. Housing developments cover the hills overlooking Highway 24 for the rest of the ride to Orinda.

San Pablo Valley grew with the coming of the California and Nevada Railroad, which reached Orinda by 1890. The railroad was plagued by washouts, however, and was sold to the Santa Fe Railroad in 1899. Today parts of the line are used

17.0 Left on Happy Valley Road. Begin 1-mile climb followed by 1.1-mile descent.

19.1 Right on Upper Happy Valley Road at stop sign.

▼

20.1 Right on El Nido Ranch Road at stop sign.

21.2 Left on Highway 24 overpass at stop sign for St. Stephens Drive.

21.3 Right on Wanda Lane at stop sign. Begin steep .2-mile climb.

21.5 Right on Muth Drive at stop sign. Begin descent.

22.3 Right on Bates Boulevard at stop sign. Begin steep .1-mile descent.

22.4 Right on Davis Road at stop sign. Davis becomes Bryant at freeway on-ramp.

22.5 Left on Moraga Way to downtown Orinda.

22.6 Ride ends at Moraga Way and Brookwood Road intersection.

■

by BART. Highway travel began to supplant the railroad as early as 1903, when a tunnel was built through the Berkeley hills. The old tunnel, 200 feet above the Caldecott Tunnel, was barely wide enough for one car. Caldecott was completed in 1937, sparking a rush of settlers and business into the San Ramon Valley.

The dam on San Pablo Creek had been envisioned as early as the 1890s for farm irrigation. Construction began in 1916 and took three years using horse-drawn scrapers. San Pablo Dam, which holds 14 billion gallons of water, was drained and reinforced in 1979 to meet state earthquake standards, at a cost of $15 million.

The reservoir contains water not only from the creek but from the Sierra Nevada as well. After a disastrous drought in 1918, water was piped from the Mokelumne River in the Sierra Nevada. The East Bay Municipal Utility District project was completed in 1929, just in time to avert another water shortage.

19. Sunol

Distance: **28 miles.**
Terrain: **Two long climbs, gentle grades.**
Traffic: **Heavy on Highway 84 and Foothill Boulevard; light elsewhere.**

This East Bay tour can be called the "Ride of Three Canyons"—Niles, Stonybrook, and Dublin. On this loop you'll see historic rail lines, scenic countryside, a little-known winery, and the western edge of Amador Valley.

Start the tour in Sunol, a rural community near Highway 84 and Interstate 680. This one-street town takes life with an easygoing sense of humor. Their honorary mayor is Bosco, a 70-pound Labrador retriever who, from time to time, wanders off and is not seen for weeks.

Sunol even has its own tourist attraction. After your bike ride you can take a step back in time and ride the Niles Canyon Railway. The Pacific Locomotive Association offers free rides (donations are gladly accepted) on old steam trains or a diesel railbus on most weekends. The association, dedicated to restoring and maintaining historic trains, has rebuilt about two miles of abandoned Southern Pacific track on the north side of Highway 84 in Niles Canyon. Their goal is to extend the track nine miles from Vallejo Mills Park in Fremont to a point outside Pleasanton. For more information write to Pacific Locomotive Association, P.O. Box 2247, Fremont, CA 94536, or phone (415) 792-6191.

Ride west down Niles Canyon for a couple of miles and turn right on Palomares Road immediately after passing under a train bridge. Traffic is moderate most times of the day on Niles Canyon

Mileage Log

0.0 Start mileage at Sunol General Store and Saloon. Ride west on Highway 84, Niles Canyon Road.

4.2 Right on Palomares Road immediately after railroad bridge.

7.0 Chouinard vineyard and winery.

8.6 Summit.

13.7 Right on Palo Verde Road at stop sign.

14.1 Right on Diablo Canyon Road at stop sign.

19.2 Name changes to Foothill Boulevard in Pleasanton.

▼

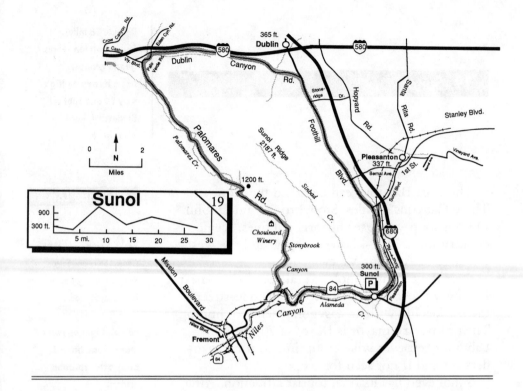

24.0 Left on Castlewood Drive at stop sign if you choose to return on Pleasanton-Sunol Road. Right again onto Pleasanton-Sunol Road after crossing bridge. Right on Highway 84, cross Arroyo de la Laguna, and then right again to return to Sunol.

27.5 End ride in Sunol.

■

Road. In contrast, Palomares Road has almost no traffic. It winds peacefully through Stonybrook Canyon next to a creek by the same name.

Several miles up the road you'll pass the Chouinard winery and vineyard on the left, owned by the Chouinard family. They offer wine tastings on weekends. Some wine is made from the on-site vineyard, which was planted in 1979. For more information call (415) 582-9900 and ask for Caroline or Damian.

Sycamore trees lining the road intermingle with madrone, dense growths of poison oak, and buckeye. At the top of the climb you can look back on the road winding down the canyon.

You'll descend a short distance into a valley with ranches, white picket fences, and cherry orchards. Leaving Palomares Road you enter Dublin Canyon

Palomares Road south of Dublin Canyon has a few cherry orchards remaining.

on Diablo Canyon Road, which parallels Interstate 580. There's a two-mile climb followed by a two-mile descent into Pleasanton.

The complexion of the ride changes from wild and scenic canyons to housing developments and large, modern office buildings in Amador Valley. The road name changes to Foothill Boulevard in Pleasanton. Traffic has increased dramatically in the past decade.

You have two options for riding to Sunol— either stay on Foothill or get on Pleasanton–Sunol Road, which is next to Arroyo de la Laguna. To reach Pleasanton–Sunol Road turn left at Castlewood Drive, cross a bridge over Arroyo de la Laguna Creek, and turn right at the next intersection. You'll have a flat ride following the creek to Highway 84. Turn right, cross Arroyo de la Laguna, and turn right again at the next intersection to return to Sunol.

Castlewood Country Club, at the intersection of Castlewood Drive and Foothill, was built by Phoebe A. Hearst, mother of publisher William

Randolph Hearst. She called this lavish resort "Rancho el Valle de San Jose."

If you choose to return to Sunol on Foothill Boulevard, you'll have a gradual climb on a lightly traveled road, culminating with a panorama of Sunol Valley and Calaveras Canyon to the south.

Distance: **57 miles.**
Terrain: **Hilly.**
Traffic: **Light to moderate.**

20. Big Basin State Park

Here's a ride for cyclists who want to see the "big picture"—big redwoods, Big Basin State Park, big climbs, and big descents. From Skyline Boulevard you'll have a panorama of Santa Clara Valley and the San Lorenzo River basin.

This ride starts in downtown Saratoga, a peaceful village that was founded in 1855 by Martin McCarty. You'll climb to Saratoga Gap at the top of the Santa Cruz Mountains and then drop into Big Basin State Park. The return trip includes a stop in Boulder Creek following a climb out of Big Basin. Then you'll return to Skyline Boulevard by Bear Creek Road and loop back to Highway 9.

It's a seven-mile climb up Highway 9 to 2,634 feet, with a steady gradient of 7 percent. The road parallels Saratoga Creek for several miles. A few miles up the road on the right there's a campground called Congress Springs. When it opened in 1866 it attracted people from all over the world. A mineral spring near the creek was believed to have curative properties. Three miles from Saratoga on the left you'll find a driveway to Congress Springs Vineyards, one of many small vineyards situated in the Santa Cruz Mountains. The winery has one of the older vineyards in Santa Clara Valley, established in the 1890s by French immigrant Pierre Pourroy. The main building was erected in 1923.

At the summit there's a parking lot with a view of Santa Clara Valley. On weekends you can find a food vendor here. The Skyline-to-the-Sea trailhead

Mileage Log

0.0 Start mileage at intersection of 4th Street and Highway 9 in downtown Saratoga. Parking available at Wildwood Park on 4th Street. Ride west on Highway 9.

0.5 Hakone Japanese Gardens on left. Road extremely steep.

1.5 Pierce Road junction on right.

3.0 Congress Springs Winery on left.

3.3 Dog City.

3.9 Redwood Gulch Road junction on right.

7.0 Continue over Skyline Boulevard junction at stop sign.

▼

13.1 Highway 236 junction. Continue straight (keeping right) on 236.

16.2 Summit.

17.8 China Grade junction.

18.9 Service Road on right at gate.

21.3 Big Basin Park headquarters on left with restrooms and water. Food and drink 50 yards on right. 236 turns south from park headquarters.

24.5 Summit.

28.0 Jamison Creek Road junction on right.

30.6 Left on Highway 9 at stop sign junction in Boulder Creek.

30.7 Right on Bear Creek Road immediately after crossing Boulder Creek Bridge.

35.1 Begin 4.7-mile climb.

39.5 David Bruce and Bear Creek Wineries.

39.8 Summit.
▼

is near the southwest corner of the intersection. It follows the old Saratoga Toll Road south of Highway 9 for several miles before crossing the highway and continuing on the north side. Bicycles are prohibited on the toll road.

Cross Skyline Boulevard and begin the six-mile descent on Highway 9 to the junction of Highway 236 at Waterman Gap. Highway 236 is a lightly traveled, narrow, curvy road that climbs gradually through tan oak, manzanita, and bay laurel. It was built in the early 1900s to reach Big Basin State Park. You'll pass China Grade junction with a view of Eagle Rock and Big Basin to the west before the final descent.

Big Basin State Park, founded in 1902, has the largest stand of old-growth redwoods in the Santa Cruz Mountains. About 3,500 of the park's 16,000 acres contain old redwoods, some more than 1,000 years old. Fifty yards north of park headquarters there's a small food store, snack bar, and museum. In a redwood tree next to the store you can often see a number of woodpeckers and Steller's jays waiting for a handout.

Head south on Highway 236, where you'll climb out of the basin and then descend for five miles into Boulder Creek. Built around the logging industry at the turn of the century, today it's a woodsy town with rustic charm. Turn left onto Highway 9 (there's a grocery corner at the junction), cross Boulder Creek, and immediately turn right on Bear Creek Road. You begin an easy climb up a forested valley for two miles before the road steepens to a constant 9 percent grade. Bear Creek Road was built in 1875 as a toll road. Santa Cruz County bought the road in 1890 for $500. From the ridgetop it's a short distance to Skyline Boulevard. During the stair-step climb to Black Road, you'll have views of both the San Lorenzo River basin and the Santa Clara Valley.

Skyline Boulevard becomes a broad two-lane road at Black Road. You're not through climbing until you've reached Mt. Bielawski on the left, about 3,000 feet in altitude. Shortly after the summit you'll pass the entrance to Castle Rock State Park on the left, a popular hiking and climbing area. It's all downhill the last nine miles into Saratoga. Ride carefully.

40.1 **Left on Skyline Boulevard. Watch carefully for road.**

43.9 Black Road junction on right. Road widens.

47.2 Summit at 3,000 feet.

47.7 Castle Rock Park entrance. No facilities.

50.3 **Right on Highway 9.**

57.3 End of ride in Saratoga.

■

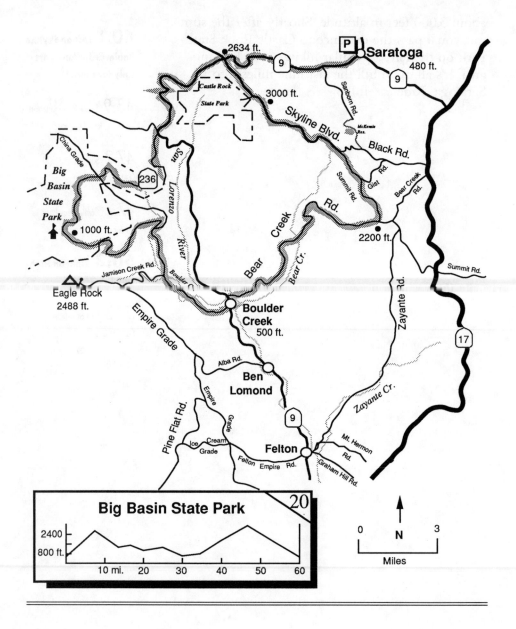

2634 ft.

P Saratoga
480 ft.

9

9

Castle Rock
State Park

3000 ft.

Skyline Blvd.

Sanborn Rd.

McKenzie Res.

Black Rd.

China Grade

Big Basin State Park

236

San Lorenzo River

Summit Rd.

Gist Rd.

Bear Creek Rd.

Bear Creek Rd.

2200 ft.

1000 ft.

Jamison Creek Rd.

Boulder C.

Bear Cr.

Summit Rd.

Eagle Rock
2488 ft.

Empire Grade

Boulder Creek
500 ft.

Zayante Rd.

17

Alba Rd.

Ben Lomond

Empire Grade

Zayante Cr.

Pine Flat Rd.

Ice Cream Grade

9

Felton Empire Rd.

Felton

Mt. Hermon Rd.

Graham Hill Rd.

Big Basin State Park

20

2400
800 ft.

10 mi.   20   30   40   50   60

0   N   3

Miles

21. Los Altos Hills

Distance: **19 miles.**
Terrain: **Hilly.**
Traffic: **Light.**

Even when Stanford University opened its doors in 1891 the bicycle played an important part in the day-to-day life of its students and residents. Bikes have changed greatly since the days of the highwheeler, the roads at Stanford are paved, and we now have cars, but the bicycle has never been more popular. Thousands of cyclists ply the many miles of roads and paths on the sprawling campus. However, a severe infestation of puncture vine prevails along the roads and causes more flat tires than all other causes combined: do not stray from the paved paths or you'll greatly increase your chances of a flat. Puncture vine spreads in a circle from a central root and has delicate yellow flowers and frilly green leaves. Unlike spike weed, a plant with obvious thorns that don't cause flats, puncture vine grows flat on the ground.

Surrounded by Palo Alto, Stanford University lies at the base of rolling oak-covered foothills. Its impressive sandstone buildings with distinctive red-tile roofs dating back to the turn of the century give visible expression to founder Leland Stanford's dream of creating a prestigious, world-renowned college.

This ride starts at the Stanford stadium, goes through the fashionable Los Altos Hills, and returns on Alpine Road. Stanford stadium has plenty of parking except during football games that are played at home (Saturdays).

Palm Drive, the main entrance to the campus, is bordered by mature palm trees. Straight ahead

Mileage Log

0.0 Start mileage at Angell Field (next to Stanford Stadium) at intersection of Galvez Drive and Campus Drive East on Stanford University campus. Ride north on Campus Drive East.

0.3 Left on Palm Drive at stop sign. Keep right when road splits.

0.8 Left on Serra Street at stop sign. Inner Quadrangle located directly west of bus stop on Serra Street. Walk bike through Inner Quadrangle to visit Stanford Church. Continue south on Serra past Hoover Tower and fountain.

1.3 Right on Campus Drive East at stop sign.

▼

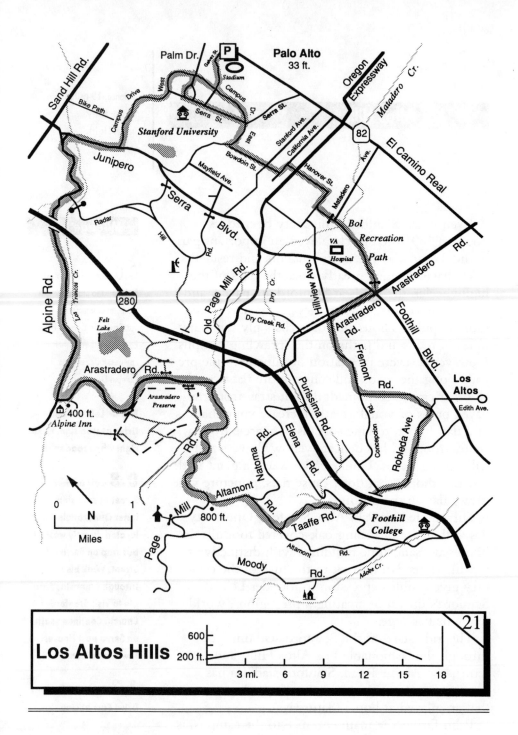

Palm Dr.

Palo Alto
33 ft.

P

Stadium

Sand Hill Rd.

Bike Path

West

Campus

Drive

Campus

Serra St.

Serra St.

Stanford Ave.

California Ave.

Stanford University

East

Serra St.

Dr.

Mayfield Ave.

Bowdoin St.

Hanover St.

Oregon Expressway

Matadero Cr.

82

El Camino Real

Ave.

Juniper o

Serra

Blvd.

Radar

Hill

Rd.

Old Page Mill Rd.

Dry Cr.

Dry Creek Rd.

Matadero

VA
Hospital

Bol
Recreation

Path

Hillview Ave.

Arastradero

Rd.

Arastradero
Rd.

Fremont

Rd.

Foothill

Blvd.

Alpine Rd.

Los Trancos Cr.

Felt
Lake

280

Arastradero   Rd.

Arastradero
Preserve

400 ft.

Alpine Inn

Rd.

Purissima Rd.

Concepcion

Rd.

Robleda Ave.

**Los
Altos**

Edith Ave.

0   1

N

Miles

Page   Mill

800 ft.

Altamont

Natoma   Rd.

Rd.

Elena

Rd.

Taaffe Rd.

Altamont   Rd.

Moody

Rd.

Adobe Cr.

**Foothill
College**

| 21 |

Los Altos Hills

600

200 ft.

3 mi.   6   9   12   15   18

you'll see the "quadrangle" and Stanford Memorial Church. Don't miss looking inside, although there are sometimes weddings or Sunday morning services. Stanford's wife, Jane, built the church in memory of her husband in 1903. Leland Stanford was a wealthy merchant and one of four men who founded the transcontinental Central Pacific Railroad. He also served as president of the Southern Pacific Railroad and was a U.S. Senator from 1885 until his death in 1893.

Those distinctive sandstone blocks used to construct the university's buildings were shipped by rail from a quarry in south San Jose. They didn't hold up well in the 1906 earthquake (especially the church, which was also damaged in the 1989 Loma Prieta earthquake), so many of the buildings have been reinforced. The quadrangle's courtyard was paved with new brick in the mid-1980s.

Continue south, passing the missile-shaped Hoover Tower, and leave campus on Bowdoin Street. At Page Mill Road the character of the ride changes briefly from residential to industrial. Two of the peninsula's best known electronics and computer companies, Hewlett-Packard and Varian, are located at the corner of Hanover Street and Page Mill.

Start riding on the recreation path that goes behind Varian and into Boll Park, a narrow grassy area bordered by Matadero Creek. You'll pass the Veterans' Hospital on the right and Gunn High School on the left. Until the late 1950s this path was a rail line for Southern Pacific, heading south from the park along what is now Foothill Expressway.

You'll start a steady but gradual climb on Arastradero Road and enter Los Altos Hills at Fremont Road. The rural community was incorporated in 1956 to guard against rampant growth. Two steps taken by the new town to limit growth included setting a lot size limit of one acre and banning any commercial business.

Take Taaffe Road, named for the family that

1.6 Left on Bowdoin Street at stop sign. Continue straight at stop sign on Stanford Avenue.

2.3 Left on California Avenue at stop sign.

2.4 Right on Hanover Street at stop sign. Cross Page Mill Road at traffic light.

3.0 Left on bike path next to Varian building. Continue south through Bol Park on path.

4.2 Right on Arastradero Road, crossing Foothill Expressway at traffic light.

4.8 Left on Fremont Road at stop sign.

5.8 Left at stop sign, staying on Fremont.

6.6 Right on Robleda Avenue. Begin climb to Page Mill Road.

7.8 Purissima Road. Turn right if you want to cut short ride and eliminate hills. Turn right on Arastradero at stop sign and retrace route.

▼

8.0 Right on Elena Road at stop sign.

8.2 Left on Taaffe Road.

9.1 Right on Altamont Road at stop sign.

10.1 Right on Page Mill Road at stop sign. Begin descent.

12.0 Left on Arastradero Road.

14.0 Right on Alpine Road at stop sign.

17.0 Right on Junipero Serra Boulevard at traffic light.

17.4 Left on Campus Drive West.

18.9 Left on Galvez Drive. End of ride.

■

once owned 3,000 acres in the area, up a scenic ridge overlooking an apricot orchard and valley. The climb steepens in the last few hundred yards before reaching Altamont Road. After some ups and downs on Altamont, turn right and begin a windy descent on Page Mill Road.

Turn left on Arastradero Road, which has one climb of about a half-mile. The road was built in the 1830s as a shortcut for wagon teams hauling lumber to the port of Alviso. The huge tree stumps on either side of the road are what remain of old eucalyptus trees that burned in a 1985 fire. The fire swept over the hills and destroyed several houses. Arastradero Preserve, a 600-acre Palo Alto park that opened in 1987, is on the left. Hiking trails lead from Arastradero to a secluded pond. In the spring the hills are covered with golden poppies and yellow mustard grass.

Rossotti's, or Alpine Inn, at the intersection of Alpine and Arastradero roads, sells food and drink. Turn right on Alpine Road and it's all downhill to Stanford campus.

22. Mount Hamilton

Distance: **104 miles.**
Terrain: **Mountainous.**
Traffic: **Light to moderate.**

Bicycling up Mt. Hamilton in the spring is an exhilarating way to start the summer. The green hills are abloom with white, yellow, and blue wildflowers. Your destination is Lick Observatory parking lot at 4,209 feet, the highest paved road in the Bay Area. You'll have breathtaking views of the Santa Cruz Mountains and even the Sierra on a clear day.

April and May are the best months to see wildflowers. California poppies and blue lupines mix with blue larkspurs, goldfields, and red owl's clover. Look closely and you'll find wild iris and Miner's lettuce.

The road, built in 1876, winds 20 miles up the mountain with gradients around 7 percent and includes two downgrades into valleys. It was built with a mild gradient for horses hauling heavy observatory equipment. The observatory was built by James Lick, who made his fortune in real estate. It was completed in 1887, but the main telescope—a massive 36-inch refractor—was installed a year later.

With the right attitude, a conservative pace, and low gears, this is one of the most fulfilling and scenic rides in the South Bay. If you're ready for a century ride (100 miles), you can loop around the mountain's rugged eastern slope to Livermore, returning on Calaveras Road. Be sure about your decision at the summit, as the road is steeper on the east slope.

The ride starts on a residential street off

Mileage Log

0.0 Start mileage in Milpitas on Calaveras Boulevard at Calaveras Court, one block east of North Victoria Drive. Ride east on Calaveras Boulevard.

0.6 Right on Piedmont Road at stop sign.

4.4 Left on Penitencia Creek Road at stop sign.

4.9 Right on Toyon Avenue.

5.8 Left on McKee Road at stop sign.

6.3 Left on Alum Rock Avenue at stop sign.

6.6 Right on Mt. Hamilton Road.

▼

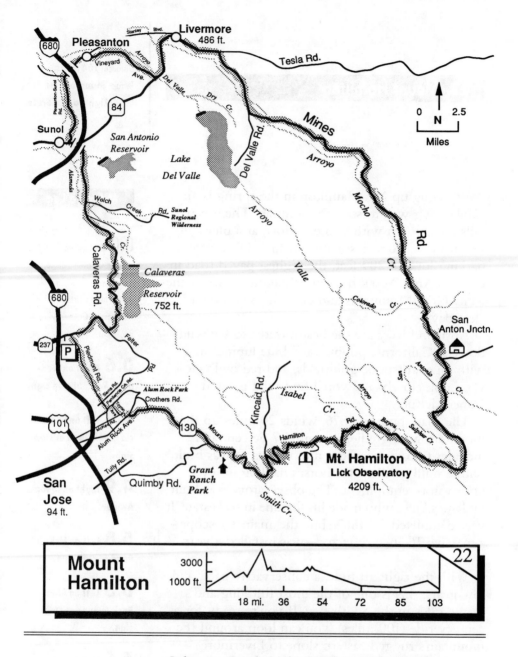

Mount Hamilton	3000					**22**
	1000 ft.					
		18 mi.	36	54	72	85 103

8.4 Crothers Road junction on left. Descends to Alum Rock Park.

▼

Calaveras Boulevard in Milpitas. You'll ride through residential flatlands for several miles before beginning to climb. After the first descent, you'll find a convenient stop at Grant Ranch

The white domes of Mt. Hamilton observatory are visible throughout Santa Clara Valley.

County Park. It has restrooms, drinking fountains, and an old ranch house and museum featuring early-California farm equipment at park headquarters. Halls Valley to the south becomes a carpet of white flowers in spring. Watch for hawks, kites, turkey vultures, bluebirds, kingbirds, woodpeckers, horned larks, and golden eagles. On a warm day you may see a badger or a roadrunner dart across

12.5 Begin 1.8-mile descent.

14.0 Quimby Road on right. Goes to San Jose.

▼

14.2 Grant Ranch County Park on right. Restrooms, fountain, history museum.

17.5 Begin .9-mile descent to Smith Creek.

19.8 Kincaid Road on left.

20.7 Giant manzanita on left.

24.7 Summit. Water available from faucet outside house on right. Observatory uphill to right. Public display open most days. View point.

25.5 Begin descent.

27.6 Emergency water from spring on right.

29.9 End of descent at Isabel Creek. Begin .6-mile climb followed by 1-mile descent.

33.1 Begin .3-mile climb.

36.2 Begin .8-mile climb followed by .7-mile descent.

38.0 San Antonio Valley flower display.

42.8 San Anton Junction bar. Keep left. Del Puerto Canyon Road on right goes to Patterson.

▼

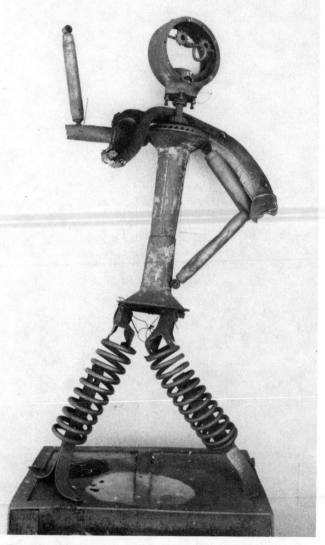

"Car Man" at San Anton Junction east of Mt. Hamilton was made from spare parts.

the road. The park is the site of a mountain bike race in the summer and off-road riding is allowed on its old ranch roads.

From Halls Valley you'll begin the middle portion of the climb through dense growths of oak. On the third climb leaving Smith Creek there are giant manzanita, a bush identified by its polished, dark cinnamon-colored limbs. The last six-mile climb has many hairpin turns and the best views. Lick Observatory staff housing and five white domes are located at the summit. Turn right to reach the observatory, open to the public on weekends from 1 to 5 p.m. The post office lobby at the north end of the observatory, with drinking fountains and restrooms, is open all day.

The east summit, Copernicus Peak, has a fire watchtower and a grand view of the Sierra as well as of Isabel Creek nearly 4,000 feet below. On the eastern side of the mountain, San Antonio Valley is carpeted with wildflowers in the early spring. The only residents in this wild, rugged country are a few ranchers and miners, with occasional sightseers, birders, survivalists and cyclists.

There's a four-mile descent to Isabel Creek and then some rolling hills as the road parallels Arroyo Bayou Creek. The old road used to follow the creekbed and had two fords, but it was moved to a higher elevation to avoid flooding.

San Anton Junction is the only food stop until Livermore. The junction bar has picnic tables where you can enjoy the lunch you wisely packed along. Or you might want to step inside and listen to the juke box, shoot pool, and quaff a cold soda from the bar. The menu includes a variety of entrees, ranging from chili to hamburgers and candy bars.

Continue on Mines Road to Livermore as it follows Arroyo Mocho Creek. You have a two-mile and a one-mile climb ahead before beginning a long, gradual descent to Livermore Valley, where vineyards dominate the landscape. Ride through Livermore and continue northwest on Vineyard Avenue to Pleasanton. Ride through town and take Pleasanton-Sunol Road to Highway 84. Turn left and begin riding up Calaveras Road.

In the late afternoon Calaveras Road has little

43.9 Begin 1.9-mile climb.

46.9 Begin 1.1-mile climb.

50.9 Alameda County Line. Sprint! Road name changes to Mines Road.

62.5 Begin 3.5-mile descent.

67.1 Right on Mines Road at stop sign.

70.6 Left on Tesla Road at stop sign, which becomes South Livermore Avenue in .1 miles.

72.1 Left on College Avenue across the street from Livermore City Hall and police station.

73.3 Left on South 4th Street at stop sign.

73.4 Left at traffic light on Holmes Street.

74.3 Shopping center with gas station, liquor store, and grocery store.

75.5 Keep right on Highway 84.

75.8 Right on Vineyard Avenue.
▼

80.0 Left on Bernal Avenue at stop sign.

80.1 Right on Vineyard Avenue at stop sign.

80.9 Left on First Street at traffic light.

82.9 Left on Pleasanton-Sunol Road after passing under Interstate 680.

86.5 Left on Highway 84 at stop sign.

87.2 Pass under Interstate 680. Becomes Calaveras Road.

87.5 Cork oak trees on right.

91.2 Start climb. False summit at 94.1 miles.

100.8 Summit.

101.2 Right on Calaveras Road at stop sign.

102.0 Ed Levin Park. Water fountains, restrooms.

104.2 End ride at Calaveras Court.

■

traffic and you'll enjoy views of the blue reservoir as you wind up to the final ridge at 1,000 feet. From here it's all downhill to complete the 104-mile sojourn.

II. Off-road Rides

23. Briones Park

Distance: **15 miles.**
Terrain: **Hilly.**
Traffic: **Cows, hikers, equestrians, bicyclists.**

Briones Regional Park north of Walnut Creek is an island of open space surrounded by country estates and ranches. But the park is so big that some hilltops offer vistas without any signs of civilization. The park's wide valleys, high ridges, and deep canyons make mountain bike riding challenging and fun.

Almost all of the old ranch roads winding through the park, shown as hiking trails on park maps, are open for bicycling. A mountain bike race has been held for several years at the park. Volunteer trail work and participation in park meetings by the Coast Range Riders have helped keep the park open to bicycling. There is a $2 fee for cars on weekends.

There are more than 5,000 acres to explore at Briones; the ride described here is one of many options. On it you'll visit all corners of the park and the central ridges. Several climbs have "walls" that require walking even by "mountain goat riders" with extra-low gears.

Most trails are marked at intersections, but with so many junctions it's easy to miss a turn. Trail conditions vary from wide dirt roads to grassy paths. In wet spots cows sometimes muddy the trail.

This tour begins at the Bear Creek Road staging area, which has a water fountain and restroom. Ride north from the parking lot on Abrigo Valley Trail as you climb steadily along a stream through a tree-covered canyon. The road takes you to a

Mileage Log

0.0 Start mileage at the Bear Creek entrance to Briones Regional Park off Bear Creek Road. The parking lot is about a half-mile from Bear Creek Road. Ride north on Abrigo Valley Trail.

0.9 Left at junction with Mott Peak Trail.

1.4 Maud Walen Camp on right.

1.9 Right on Briones Crest Trail.

2.2 Right on Briones Crest Trail at Lagoon Trail junction.

3.0 Left on Lagoon Trail.

3.6 Right on Toyon Canyon Trail.

▼

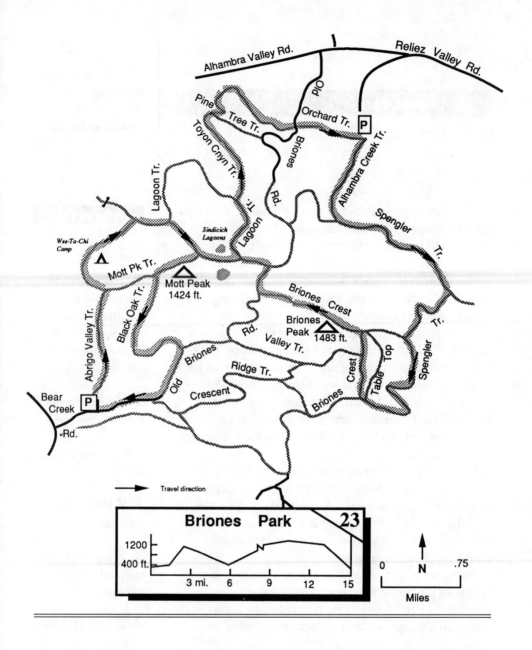

Alhambra Valley Rd.

Reliez Valley Rd.

Pine Tree Tr.

Toyon Cnyn Tr.

Old Orchard Tr.

P

Alhambra Creek Tr.

Briones Rd.

Lagoon Tr.

Lagoon Tr.

Sindicich Lagoons

Spengler Tr.

Wee-Ta-Chi Camp

Mott Pk Tr.

Black Oak Tr.

Mott Peak
1424 ft.

Briones Crest

Briones Peak
1483 ft.

Abrigo Valley Tr.

Old Briones Rd.

Valley Tr.

Ridge Tr.

Briones Crest

Table Top

Spengler Tr.

Bear Creek

P

Crescent

Briones

Rd.

Travel direction

Briones Park **23**

1200

400 ft.

3 mi.   6   9   12   15

0   N   .75

Miles

4.6 **Left on Pine Tree Trail.**

▼

beautiful valley with a meadow and picnic area at Wee-Ta-Chi Camp. It's a quiet, pastoral setting among giant bay trees.

The trail gets narrow and steep beyond the camp. After a hairpin turn, continue to a ridge

This is just one of the impressive views you'll have in Briones Park.

with a grand view of Mt. Diablo, Benicia-Martinez Bridge, Mt. Tamalpais, and Mt. St. Helena to the north.

Descending Briones Crest Trail you'll see two small ponds that almost always have water. They're a gathering place for wildlife, including deer, raccoons, skunks, and bobcats. Sindicich Lagoon on Lagoon Trail is surrounded by a fence to keep cattle out. There's a long bumpy descent on Toyon Canyon Trail and Pine Tree Trail, named for the trees that grow here.

Orchard Trail is the site of a former orchard and ranch. A few fruit trees remain. Coulter pines, with their huge cones more than a foot long and weighing two pounds, grow near the orchard.

Cross paved Old Briones Road and descend to a wide valley, where you'll find the park's northern entrance, Alhambra Creek Valley Staging Area. Alhambra Creek Trail takes you up a valley cloaked in blue lupine in the spring. Climbing steadily through the oaks and bay laurels along the creek, you'll come to Spengler Trail and climb

4.7 Right on Orchard Trail.

5.3 Cross Old Briones Road at Rancho Briones.

5.9 Right on Alhambra Creek Trail at Alhambra Creek Valley Staging Area. Drinking fountain and restrooms.

6.9 Left on Spengler Trail.

7.9 Right at junction with Blue Oak Trail.

8.7 Left at junction staying on Spengler Trail.

▼

10.0 Right onto
Spengler Trail. Dirt road
goes to service area.

10.4 Right on Table
Top Trail.

11.1 Left on Briones
Crest Trail.

12.0 Right at
Lagoon Trail junction.

12.1 Left on Briones
Crest Trail.

12.6 Left on Mott
Peak Trail.

13.0 Left on Black
Oak Trail.

14.0 Right on Old
Briones Road.

14.8 Ride ends at Bear
Creek parking lot.

■

through a beautiful stand of oak trees. After a descent, climb the first wall; it lasts about 200 yards. Turn left and stay on Spengler Trail. You'll have a view of ranch houses in the canyon below. Drop into a gully and assault the next wall to a ridge, where there's more climbing.

Take a hard right at the gate to join Table Top Trail. After a roller coaster hill you'll come to a communications tower and then ride through a wide meadow covered with poppies in the spring. To the right there's a panorama of Suisun Bay, and on a clear day you can see the Sierra. Most of the climbing is over now. Table Top intersects Briones Crest Trail. Ride down to Lagoon Trail, climb the hill you rode down earlier, and take a left onto Mott Peak Trail, which runs along the top of a narrow ridge and over Mott Peak at 1,424 feet. Descend Black Oak Trail and hold onto your hat for a steep, bumpy descent to Old Briones Road. Turn right here and ride back to the Bear Creek staging area.

Briones Park opened in 1967. Prior to becoming a park the land was used for ranching and cattle grazing and served as a watershed for the San Pablo Dam. The earliest settler was Felipe Briones, who built a home in 1829 near the Bear Creek entrance. His land was part of the huge "Rancho Boca de la Cañada del Pinole" Mexican land grant. During Prohibition these isolated ranchlands were the site of bootlegging.

24. The Forest of Nisene Marks State Park

Distance: **38 miles.**
Terrain: **Hilly.**
Traffic: **Bicycles, equestrians, hikers.**

Every off-road rider dreams of the ultimate descent, that remote forest trail winding endlessly down a mountain. The Forest of Nisene Marks State Park southeast of Santa Cruz comes close to the fantasy. You drop 2,600 feet in 13 miles on a dirt road with a steady gradient through the redwoods. But what makes this ride a classic are spectacular ocean views, a beautiful madrone forest, and creek crossings.

This mountain bike tour starts near Summit Center Store on Summit Road, about four miles south of Highway 17. It's the only place you can buy food until Aptos, so stock up now. The best riding is in the spring and early winter when the road is hardpacked. It gets dusty in the summer and muddy after heavy rain. Bring water; there isn't any along the way.

For the first eight miles you'll ride below a ridge overlooking the impressive Soquel Creek Canyon as you pass remote houses along the bumpy two-lane Highland Way. If you're wondering where Mt. Bache Road goes, it climbs steeply to Loma Prieta Mountain.

Highland Way descends gradually through scrub oak, poison oak, tan oak, bay laurel, and greasewood. After about six miles you'll ride through the upper end of Soquel Creek Canyon and follow the creek on the right. At this location one spring day cyclists rode through swarms of lady bugs.

After leaving the creek there's about a half-mile climb to the summit. Highland Way becomes

Mileage Log

0.0 Start mileage at Summit Center Store on Summit Road, 4 miles south of Highway 17. Do not park in the store lot. Ride south on Summit Road.

0.1 San Jose-Soquel Road junction.

1.9 Right at Highland Way and stop sign. Take immediate left to continue on Highland.

7.8 Right on Buzzard Lagoon Road at summit, identified by a large "prevent fires" sign. Ormsby Cutoff on left.

8.3 Left turn. Park entrance sign is just ahead.

8.7 Right turn at summit.

▼

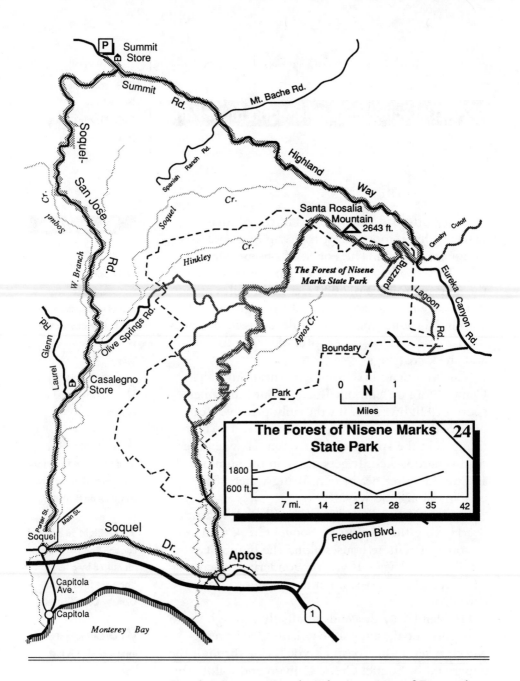

10.0 Locked fireroad gate.
Begin descent in one mile.

▼

Eureka Canyon Road at the junction of Buzzard Lagoon Road on the right and Ormsby Cutoff on the left. Turn right onto Buzzard Lagoon Road, the main dirt road, to reach Nisene Marks Park. The road climbs steadily through dense growths of tan oak and redwood. Be sure to turn right at the summit of Buzzard Lagoon Road, which goes down to Ryder Road and back to Eureka Canyon Road.

You'll circle Mount Rosalia on smooth sandstone outcroppings. Past the last gate at 10 miles Aptos Creek Fire Road levels before descending through a forest of madrone, identified by its flaky red bark and smooth green wood.

Although the road suffered several major landslides in the winter floods of 1982–83, it was repaired and is now in good shape. Watch for hikers and bicyclists on this popular road.

At the bottom of the canyon you'll cross Aptos Creek twice, first by bridge and then by fording. Look out for old railroad ties in the road before crossing the bridge.

Aptos Canyon was logged between 1883 and 1923 by the Loma Prieta Lumber Company, which built a sawmill and town near the creek. It was served by a standard gauge Southern Pacific rail seven miles into the canyon from Aptos. Some 140 million board feet of lumber later, all but a handful of old-growth redwoods had been cut down.

In 1963 Andrew Marks and Herman Agnes donated 9,600 acres of former lumber company land to the state in memory of their mother, Nisene Marks. Today the park has more than 30 miles of hiking trails and fire roads. Cyclo-cross (off-road) races are held next to the road a couple of miles east of Aptos.

The coastal community of Aptos grew around the logging industry, dating as far back as the 1830s. By the 1880s two large sawmills were situated north of town, serviced by local railroads.

You'll return on San Jose-Soquel Road (also called Old San Jose Highway). The road, which runs along Soquel Creek through apple orchards and residential areas in the lower valley, follows the original toll road built through the canyon in 1858. Highway 17 to the north wasn't built until 1916 and didn't take its present alignment until 1934.

14.3 Ocean view at Sand Point Overlook. Keep left at this junction.

20.0 Ford Aptos Creek.

20.3 Ride around locked gate at parking lot.

22.2 Pavement.

23.2 Right on Soquel Drive.

26.7 Right on Soquel-San Jose Road at stop sign.

30.0 Casalegno Store.

30.2 Rose garden on right.

37.8 Left on Summit Road at stop sign.

37.9 Return to store.

■

Aptos Creek Fire Road in the Forest of Nisene Marks park is an old logging railroad route.

Sand Point Overlook offers ocean views in The Forest of Nisene Marks State Park.

At the junction with Laurel Glen Road you'll find Casalegno Store, a classic country store. Casalegno is Italian for wooden house, but it was also the name of the store's owner, George Casalegno. Look for a beautiful rose garden on the right past the store.

25. Gazos Creek Road

Distance: **28 miles.**
Terrain: **Hilly.**
Traffic: **Hikers, bicyclists, equestrians.**

Big Basin State Park, located 20 miles northeast of Santa Cruz in the Santa Cruz Mountains, has some of the most dramatic and remote off-road riding anywhere in this region. You might call it your typical Bay Area wilderness experience.

Although all park trails were closed to bicycling in the early 1980s, bicycles are permitted on the fire roads you'll be using. This loop through Big Basin State Park and Butano State Park has something for every rider: long downhills, burbling creeks, ancient redwoods, whoop-de-doos, and a spectacular climb from near sea level to 2,200 feet. You'll even cross an airstrip on a lonely mountain ridge.

Road conditions are best in the spring; the road gets loose and dusty in the summer. In fact, Gazos Creek Road can become like a sandpit four to six inches deep. On the other hand, a tour of the road after the floods of 1982–83 amounted to an arduous hike over downed redwoods and boulders. Nearly a mile of road was wiped out by the rampaging Gazos Creek.

This tour begins at Big Basin Park headquarters. Starting on Gazos Creek Road at an altitude of 1,000 feet, you'll gradually climb 330 feet through redwoods and Douglas fir with an understory of mostly huckleberry, toyon, and tan oak. A mile-long descent is followed by another climb to 1,350 feet. You'll come to a devastated area at the bottom of the first descent. Redwoods here grow to enormous heights but have shallow roots that make

Mileage Log

0.0 Start mileage at the junction of Gazos Creek Road and North Escape Road about a quarter-mile north of Big Basin State Park headquarters on Highway 236. Gazos Creek Road immediately crosses a bridge over Opal Creek.

0.1 Locked gate.

0.9 Middle Ridge Trail on right. You'll return on this road.

3.0 Locked gate.

6.1 Sandy Point Guard Station.

6.2 Johansen Road; second gate on right after passing open area.

8.1 Locked gate at bottom of hill.

▼

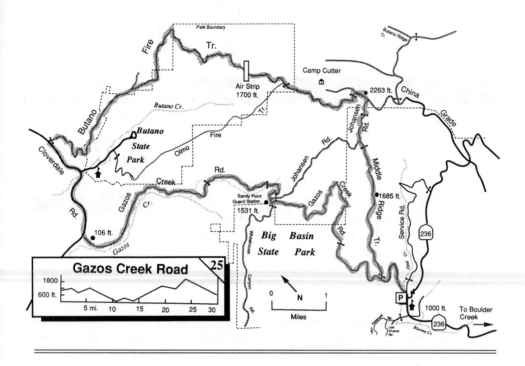

8.3 Bridge over Gazos Creek.

9.7 Log dam artifact in Gazos Creek.

11.5 Right on Cloverdale Road. Unsigned.

12.7 Butano State Park entrance. Water available .3 miles from entrance.

13.6 Right at paved ramp (Butano Fire Trail) up 15 yards to a locked aluminum gate. Unsigned.

▼

them susceptible to land movements and strong winds. This soil has lots of clay that became saturated by nearby springs and heavy rains in 1982–83. The trees toppled as the earth crept down the hill.

Six miles into the ride you'll reach Sandy Point Guard Station, a major junction in a clearing. One winter in the mid-1960s a ranger station at this site burned to the ground. Park officials speculate vagrants broke into the station and lit a gas stove that caught fire. Foundations and a few pipes are the only remains.

Now you can either turn back or continue on Gazos Creek for a steep descent. Gazos Creek Road becomes more rutted and bumpy as you descend to the creek. Until the mid-1960s, this San Mateo County road was open to car traffic.

At the bottom of the hill Gazos Creek Road becomes a well-traveled, flat dirt road that follows the creek to the ocean under a canopy of sycamore, ash, maple, and Pacific dogwood. In the late 1890s Gazos Creek had a completely different complexion. It was dammed and used as a log pen for a sawmill near the road. Remnants of the redwood dam on the banks of the creek are still visible from the road.

On Cloverdale Road you'll hit pavement for a couple of miles. The road was paved from Butano State Park to the ocean in 1987. Your next turn is not marked, so watch carefully for Butano Fire Trail where it joins Cloverdale. There's a short, steep paved driveway leading to an aluminum gate, about one mile north of the Butano park entrance. The dirt road climbs an exposed ridge before entering a wooded canyon with impressive stands of Douglas fir. The lower parts of the canyon feature dense foliage of brambles, poison oak, and blackberries.

With one exception (shown on the Mileage Log), there are no road junctions on Butano Fire Trail. You'll climb for what seems like an eternity as the terrain changes from tree-covered slopes to granulated shale. Redwoods are replaced by knobcone pines on the dry, rocky ridges. The road becomes a smooth bed of crushed white shale that leads up to an airstrip.

After crossing the airstrip you'll have a brief descent into a dark forest, followed by more climbing. Your second chance for water comes at Butano Trail Camp (there's water available in Butano State Park), where there's a fountain next to a toilet. The climb brings you to the top of the ridge at China Grade, altitude 2,265 feet. Go right; there's a Boy Scout camp to the left. Take the road (it used to be paved) to Johansen Road, the next right turn. Descend about .9 miles and turn left on Middle Ridge Trail. It's a rollercoaster ride to Gazos Creek over slabs of sandstone and through sandpits. Back on Gazos Creek Road turn left and return to park headquarters, where there's an interpretive center, snack bar, and food store.

Big Basin Park was founded in 1902 through

16.2 Keep right at junction, staying on Butano Fire Trail.

16.8 Gate, usually open.

18.7 Cross airstrip. Watch out for planes.

19.3 Butano Trail Camp on right. Water available.

19.7 Olmo Fire Road on right.

19.8 Locked gate.

22.7 Locked cable across road. Right at junction onto China Grade.

23.2 Right on Johansen Road.

24.1 Left on Middle Ridge Fire Trail.

24.3 Locked gate.

26.1 Dooly Trail.

26.6 Left on Gazos Creek Road.

27.5 Return to North Escape Road and picnic grounds.

■

the efforts of Andrew Hill, a San Jose artist and photographer. In 1900 the Sempervirens Club was founded to raise money and lobby to make this impressive stand of old-growth redwoods a state park and thereby protect it from logging. In 1968 the club was revived as the Sempervirens Fund when developers threatened to build on private land inside the park boundary. The Los Altos-based fund has raised money to help expand the park to its present size of 16,000 acres.

26. Henry Coe State Park

Distance: **16 miles.**
Terrain: **Steep.**
Traffic: **Hikers, eques-trians, bicycles.**

If you're seeking remote trails and a test of riding skills, Henry W. Coe State Park is your ticket to adventure. California's second largest state park, 20 miles southeast of San Jose, covers nearly 100 square miles. More than 200 miles of ranch roads and trails extend to the park's isolated eastern boundary. In the past several years the park has become a favorite haunt for mountain bikes.

Late fall and early spring are the best seasons for visiting. In the spring you'll see wildflowers covering open meadows among giant oaks. In the fall you'll enjoy autumn colors and cool, crisp air. Maples, sycamores, and alders lining creeks in narrow canyons turn red, yellow, and orange. It gets hot in the summer and water is extremely scarce; in fact, it's only available at park headquarters.

On this ride you'll make a figure eight loop that includes two sections of narrow trail. The rest of the ride is on wide dirt roads. Be prepared for some steep climbs and descents. Always expect to encounter other trail users around the next turn.

This ride starts at a signed gate across the road from a parking lot at the park entrance. I recommend that you stay off the single-track trail leaving park headquarters, as this is where most hikers travel. Take the dirt road for .4 miles and turn left, uphill. The road rises steeply across an open ridge. At the summit on the right there's a granite monument dedicated to Henry Coe.

Begin descending for about a mile to Frog Lake on the right. The road circles the small lake, which

Mileage Log

0.0 To reach Henry Coe Park take Highway 101 south to the Dunne Avenue exit in Morgan Hill. Go left (east) and drive up a narrow, curvy road for the next 13 miles to the park entrance. There's a $3 parking fee. Start mileage at the signed gate across from the parking lot at the park entrance, going east.

0.4 Left at dirt road to monument, uphill.

0.9 Monument on right.

1.0 Begin descent to Frog Lake. Take trail at mile 1.6 if you want to reach lake. Otherwise stay left on road.

1.9 Begin climb.

2.8 Right on Middle Ridge Trail. View point straight ahead.

▼

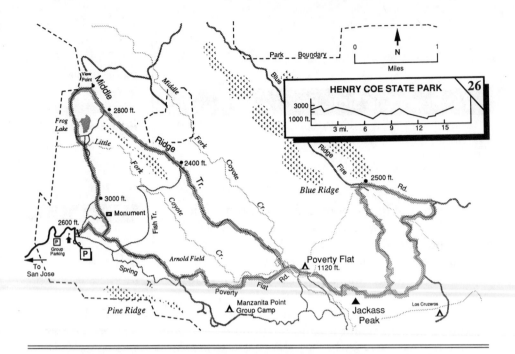

Park Boundary

HENRY COE STATE PARK **26**

View Point

Middle

Frog Lake

Little

Middle

Fork

Ridge

2800 ft.

2400 ft.

Coyote

Blue

Ridge

Fire

Rd.

2500 ft.

Blue Ridge

Fork

Little

Fork

3000 ft.

Monument

Coyote

Tr.

Cr.

2600 ft.

Fish Tr.

P

Group Parking

P

To San Jose

Spring

Tr.

Arnold Field

Cr.

Poverty Flat

1120 ft.

Poverty

Flat

Rd.

Manzanita Point Group Camp

Jackass Peak

Los Cruzeros

Pine Ridge

3.1 Frog Lake junction on right.

4.3 Fish Trail junction on right. Begin steep descent at mile 5.0.

6.4 Middle Fork Coyote Creek.

6.6 Left on Poverty Flat Road.

7.9 Trailhead on left. You'll return here.

8.1 Los Cruzeros camp junction on right.

▼

is out of sight below you. There's a gradual climb to the Deerhorn Viewpoint and Middle Ridge Trail. Middle Ridge is just before the view point on the right, at the signed stake that reads "Frog Lake." From the view point you'll see Blue Ridge and Short-Cut Road dropping precipitously. A few hardy riders have even ridden down it.

Turn around and pick up Middle Ridge Trail. The trail rolls along over the next two miles. Keep left at the two junctions, both on the right. The trail drops steeply to the Middle Fork of Coyote Creek. The rocky creekbed is fun to ford when water is running in the spring. Ride a short distance to Poverty Flat Road and turn left. From the backpack camp on Poverty Flat continue east up Jackass Peak, which has a steep climb of less than a mile. On the other side at Miller Field you'll encounter a couple of steep hills. Keep left at the three major junctions. After the third junction you'll climb Blue Ridge Road for about a mile.

To find the next narrow hiking trail, watch the

left side of the road carefully and check your bike computer (see Mileage Log). After riding through oak trees on a steep section you'll come to a flat spot with a small clearing on the left. Go west about 20 feet off the road and pick up the trail paralleling the road. Turn left on the trail and begin climbing through some oak trees. In about 50 yards you'll come to a trail post. Turn right onto the trail and continue climbing. Soon you'll reach a clearing with a splendid view of the park facing south. The trail winds down the hill through mesquite and open meadows, returning you to Miller Field and the ranch road.

Return to headquarters via Poverty Flat. Leaving Poverty Flat you'll run into two sections early on with gradients as steep as 20 percent. Then the road levels off and later climbs less steeply to Arnold Field.

You've explored only a small portion of the park. In the remote southern section I've seen wild boars. In fact, the land in the east is so wild that the state recently designated much of it a wilderness area, with bicycles prohibited. Check with park rangers to find out which roads and trails are open and ride carefully: with no medical aid available for miles, this is no place to be injured.

Before this area became a park in 1953, Henry Coe's sons and daughters used the land for cattle grazing at Pine Ridge Ranch. Sada Coe, Henry's daughter, donated the ranch to Santa Clara County. Over the years several more ranches were added to the park through donations and sales. Cattle ranching continues in the park at several private inholdings. Don't be surprised to see cattle and the occasional rancher's truck on your ride.

Overnight campgrounds near headquarters are available, or you can ride into the park to camp at designated sites. Camping reservations are on a first-come-first-served basis.

Chamise, sagebrush, and poison oak thrive on the park's many steep slopes and canyons; know what poison oak looks like and avoid it.

9.1 Keep left at junction. Begin climb on Blue Ridge Fire Road.

9.9 Left at clearing. Go 20 feet and turn left again on trail. Right at trail marker, uphill.

10.1 Begin descent.

11.3 Return to Poverty Flat Road and go right.

12.7 Begin climb.

14.4 Manzanita Point junction on left. Keep right.

16.0 End ride at park headquarters.

■

27. Lake Lagunitas

Mileage Log

0.0 Start mileage at post office on Ross Common in Ross off Sir Frances Drake Boulevard. Ride west a short distance and turn left onto Lagunitas Road.

0.8 Lagunitas Road ends at Natalie Coffin Greene Park.

1.1 Right in parking lot at wooden bridge on Phoenix Lake Road. Sign on other side of bridge points way to Mt. Tamalpais and Phoenix Lake.

1.4 Go straight at junction. Phoenix Lake dam on left. Restrooms on right.

1.5 Worn Spring Road junction. Keep left.

▼

The main attraction of the Marin water district is its sparkling blue reservoirs that comprise the Mt. Tamalpais watershed. Three of the five reservoirs are within easy riding distance from Ross: Phoenix, Bon Tempe, and Lagunitas. On this tour you'll see these reservoirs as you wind up water department service roads through the oak-wooded hills above Ross. Lagunitas was built in 1873 by William T. Coleman, who needed water to build housing for San Rafael. Phoenix was built in 1905 and Bon Tempe in 1949.

This tour starts at city park in downtown Ross. Ride to Natalie Coffin Greene Park at the end of Lagunitas Road, which is lined with giant liquid amber and Dutch elm. In the fall the road is reminiscent of fall in New England. Upon reaching the park's car lot, pick up Phoenix Lake Road behind the signed gate. After a quarter-mile of easy climbing you'll reach Phoenix Lake. Keep the lake on your left, passing Worn Spring Road to the right.

Stay on Phoenix Trail until you reach a major intersection, with Eldridge Grade on the left and Shaver Grade on the right. Continue straight up Fish Grade. It's a hustle in low gear until leveling off on a paved service road, which intersects Sky Oaks Road at the summit. You'll see Bon Tempe Lake straight ahead; cormorants and other interesting birds can often be found here.

Turn left on Sky Oaks and ride to Lake Lagunitas parking area. A right turn takes you to Fairfax.

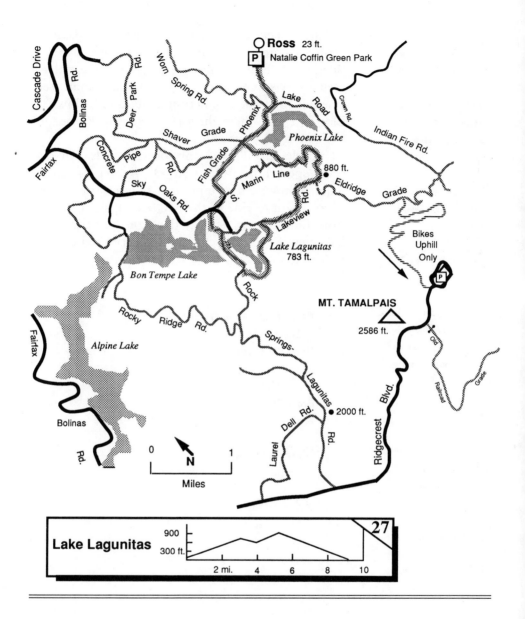

Climb a dirt road on the left to Lagunitas Dam.
Ride counterclockwise around the lake, keeping
left at junctions. Cross a wooden platform on the
other side of the dam. The southern shore has an
enjoyable dirt road through the oaks where you'll
ford two small streams. Leaving the lakeshore, turn
right on Lakeview Road and climb to Eldridge Grade.

2.1 Four-way junction. Go straight uphill on Fish Grade. Shaver Grade on right. Eldridge Grade on left. You'll return on Eldridge Grade.

2.7 Pavement. End of steep climb. South Marin Line Grade on left.

2.8 Left at Sky Oaks Road. Bon Tempe Lake.

3.1 Parking area and picnic grounds for Lake Lagunitas. Restrooms and phone on left. Take dirt road with sign that says Protection Road.

3.2 Cross dam.

3.4 Left at junction. Circle lake. Sign says Rock Spring Road.

4.3 Right on Lakeview Road.

4.6 Meadow. Non-native Coulter pine trees are being removed.

5.0 Left on Eldridge Grade Trail.

5.7 Left at junction, downhill.

Circle back to the trail intersection you passed earlier, where Shaver Grade and Phoenix Lake Road meet. Eldridge has a gradual descent with scenic views of Richardson Bay and San Francisco. There is one crucial junction about a mile down Eldridge. Take the right fork; the left fork goes back up to Sky Oaks Road.

Bicycles are allowed only on fire roads. The district's speed limit is 15 mph. District regulations require slowing to 5 mph to pass other trail users. If you want to ride to the Mt. Tamalpais summit from Eldridge Grade, take the right fork from Lakeview Road. Bicycles are not permitted down Eldridge, so have an alternate route prepared.

6.2 Right, downhill on Eldridge Grade, at Marin Line Grade.

7.0 Right on Fish Grade-Phoenix Lake Road.

9.0 Right at Ross Common.

9.1 End of ride.

■

28. Mount Tamalpais

Distance: **22 miles.**
Terrain: **Hilly.**
Traffic: **Cars, bicycles, hikers, equestrians.**

Once you take a ride on the Old Railroad Grade up Mt. Tamalpais you'll understand why the modern mountain bike originated here in the mid-1970s.

No one person can be called the inventor of the mountain bike, but Joe Breeze, Gary Fisher, Charlie Kelly, Otis Guy, and Marc Vendetti made important contributions, and they all lived within a few miles of the mountain. Their first mountain bikes were old one-speed balloon-tire bikes. Within a decade the mountain bike had become a multi-million-dollar industry. Joe Breeze built the first successful modern mountain bike frame in 1977.

Cyclists living at the base of the mountain extending from Mill Valley to Fairfax have off-road riding opportunities right at their back doors. Many trails and roads lead to the railroad grade, which snakes its way up the mountain in a series of 281 curves.

This mountain bike tour starts in Marin City at a large parking lot under Highway 101. You'll ride north through Mill Valley, pick up the railroad grade to West Point, head to the ocean, and return on Highway 1 via Tennessee Valley in the Golden Gate National Recreation Area.

The Old Railroad Grade is a smooth dirt road with only a few rocky sections. The trail is popular with hikers and bicyclists year round. The speed limit is 15 mph, 5 mph when passing other trail users.

About the only visible remnant of the railroad is

Mileage Log

0.0 Start at the parking area under Highway 101's Richardson Bay Bridge. To get there take the Stinson Beach Highway 1 exit and take first right on Pohono Street, then left through parking lot for office buildings.

0.2 Take bike path and cross over Coyote Creek inlet.

0.5 Left at crosswalk, then immediate right on Miller Avenue in bike lane. Continue through El Camino Alto stop light. Tamalpais High School on left.

2.1 Right on Presidio at green bike lane sign. Then right on Forest at dead end.

2.3 Left on East Blithedale Avenue at stop sign.

▼

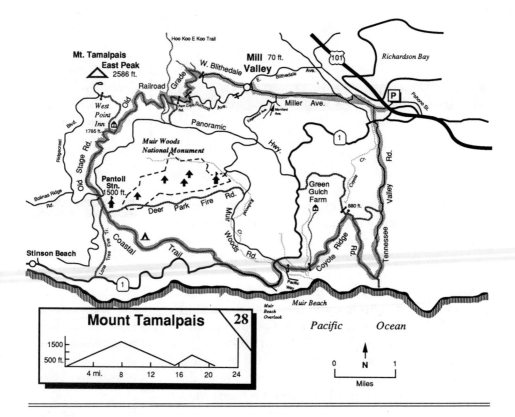

2.5 Straight on East
Blithedale. Do not turn
left.

2.8 Left. Becomes
West Blithedale Avenue.

3.6 Right at Fire
Road gate just past Lee
Street onto the Old Rail-
road Grade. The sign
says "Blithedale
Summit."

▼

a concrete platform (Mesa Junction Station) 6.8
miles into the ride at the junction to Muir Woods.
Farther up at mile 8.2 there was a water tower fed
by Fern Canyon Falls, where you can still get a
drink.

West Point Inn, built in 1904, lies at an important trail junction. If you go right, it's about a
mile-and-a-half to the summit, where there's a
concession stand that's usually open in the summer. Keep left at West Point and go to the Pan Toll
Station to pick up the Coastal Fire Trail. The
descent to Highway 1 features lovely ocean panoramas. Go left on Highway 1 and descend to Redwood Creek and the Pelican Inn, a restaurant-bar
modeled after an English pub. You'll climb steeply
from Muir Beach to Coyote Ridge. At the ridge
trail junction go right and descend to Tennessee

Joe Breeze rides his aluminum mountain bike on the Coastal Fire Trail in Mt. Tamalpais State Park.

Valley Road on a wide fire road. It's a flat ride through the valley to Highway 1.

The Mill Valley & Mt. Tamalpais Railway that went to the mountain summit was founded in early 1896 by Sidney Cushing. It was completed in August of that year after numerous objections and lawsuits by Mill Valley residents (who didn't want their quiet streets ripped up for the railway) had been overcome. The 8.25-mile line with gradients between 5 and 7 percent extended from Mill Valley to the summit, where there was a hotel built by the railroad to wine and dine overnight guests. The railroad was a popular tourist attraction but hardly a financial windfall for its owners. It weathered the lean years, however, and even extended its line to Muir Woods, which became a national monument in 1909.

Visitors from all over the world came to take the excursion. Small but powerful Shay locomotives pushed passenger cars to the summit. A later attraction included gravity cars that glided silently down the mountain through the redwoods to Muir Woods. In the summer Bay Area residents liked to take the train to West Point Inn six miles up the mountain and then walk to the Mt. Tamalpais outdoor theater.

3.8 Right onto Blithedale Ridge Road if you want to take alternate route up to Mt. Tamalpais.

4.3 Left at junction, down dip in road, and across creek. Site of Horseshoe Bend Trestle.

5.1 McKinley Cut. Rock had to be blasted here to lay track. Named for President McKinley, who visited this site.

5.4 Right on Fern Canyon Road at top of Summit Avenue, paved.

6.1 End of pavement, railroad grade continues at gate.

6.5 Right at junction with Muir Woods branch of old railway (first bend of Double Bow Knot) then immediately right again.

6.9 Left at junction with Hoo-Koo-E-Koo Trail (second bend of Double Bow Knot).

7.9 Fern Canyon Falls. Train water tower was located here.

▼

8.8 West Point Inn. Right at junction to continue to east summit of Mt. Tam (1.4 miles). Left to Old Stage Road. Water fountain at junction.

9.3 Pavement. Water fountain.

9.8 Left across Panoramic Highway to Pan Toll park headquarters and parking area. Water fountain and restrooms. Go straight on paved road past parking area on right and begin Coastal Fire Trail.

10.3 Lone Tree Road junction on right. Keep left.

10.4 Deer Park Fire Road junction on left. Keep right.

10.6 Overlook on right.

11.8 Shansky Backpack Camp on left.

12.7 Iris plantings both sides of trail. Do not touch.

Automobiles, buses, and the Great Depression spelled doom for the railroad. So did the 1924 completion of Ridgecrest Boulevard to the Mt. Tam summit. The death knell came when a fire swept the mountain in 1929, destroying the hotel and a locomotive. A year later the rails were removed and the right-of-way turned over to hikers.

12.8 Right at two round wood posts with gap in fence to Coast Highway. Descend past Muir Beach Overlook on right and Muir Woods Road on left at right bend in road.

15.6 Right at Pacific Way. Pelican Inn on corner.

15.7 Left at aluminum gate.

15.9 Left through gate at Muir Beach Lagoon. Right at next junction up steep hill on dirt road, 200 yards from gate. Left junction goes to Green Gulch Farm and Zen Center.

16.2 Coastal Trail on right.

16.3 Right at gate and continue straight up hill along fence.

17.4 Right at junction on top of Coyote Ridge. Right again in 100 yards on dirt road.

18.6 Coastal Trail on right.

19.2 Left at bottom of hill in Tennessee Valley. Pavement begins in .3 miles.

19.8 Miwok Stables and parking lot.

21.5 Highway 1 and Tennessee Valley Road junction. Ride across gravel parking lot on left and take trail under Highway 1 bridge. Becomes paved recreation path on other side.

21.7 Right on recreation path at junction.

21.8 End ride at parking lot under Highway 101.

■

Distance: **18 miles.**
Terrain: **Hilly.**
Traffic: **Light: pedestrians, equestrians, bicycles.**

29. Old Haul Road

Deep in the redwoods in San Mateo County there's a little-known recreation path built on a railroad right-of-way that's perfect for exploring by bicycle. Of course you won't see a train today, only the occasional hiker and horseback rider. The tracks and the train—a 42-ton oil-burning Shay that hauled logs to the Santa Cruz Lumber Company mill near Waterman Gap—served for 30 years, from 1921 to '51. Log trucks did the work of the train until 1972, when the mill was shut down.

In 1970 public agencies bought half of Santa Cruz Lumber's forest lands and established them as Pescadero Creek Park in San Mateo County. The park's southern boundary borders Portola State Park, which was founded in 1945. Pescadero's 7,000 acres have many miles of hiking trails that link with Portola State Park's 2,400 acres of redwoods.

In the spring yellow-flowered Western broom creates an enchanting corridor on the Old Haul Road, with different views around every bend. Numerous brooks trickle down Butano Ridge to join Pescadero Creek. During the winter of 1982–83 these peaceful streams became raging torrents, uprooting redwoods and destroying the road. In 1984 work crews from the sheriff's honor farm, located in the park, pitched in to repair the road and clear brush. Today the road is hard-packed with numerous graveled sections, making it ridable all year round. Trail signs greet you at every road and junction.

Mileage Log

0.0 Start mileage at Old Haul Road Trailhead on Wurr Road, next to Memorial County Park, near Loma Mar. Trailhead is .3 miles south of Pescadero Road and about a half-mile north of Memorial Park entrance. Ride north toward Pescadero Road.

0.3 Right on Pescadero Road at stop sign.

3.0 Haskins Hill summit.

3.8 Entrance to Sam McDonald County Park.

4.3 Right on Alpine Road.

5.6 Heritage Grove old-growth redwoods on right.

6.0 Begin Alpine Road ascent.

▼

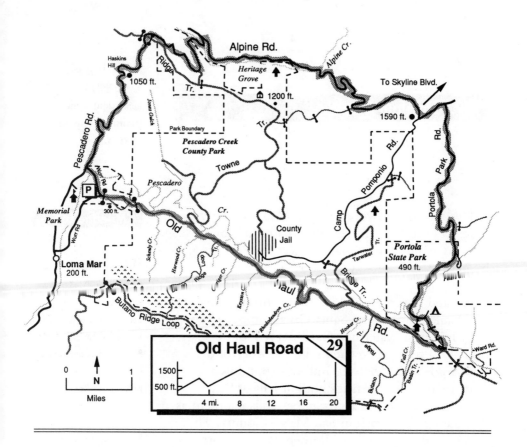

Old Haul Road 29

1500
500 ft.

4 mi. 8 12 16 20

8.0 Pomponio Road junction. Keep left.

8.4 Right on Portola Park Road at stop sign. Begin descent.

10.6 Portola State Park boundary.

11.8 Park headquarters and interpretive center. Restrooms and water.

▼

This ride starts next to Memorial Park near Loma Mar. The park has picnic grounds, camping, and a swimming area. You'll also find restrooms and water fountains here. On this loop you'll take Pescadero and Alpine roads, returning via Portola State Park and the Old Haul Road. A less strenuous alternative is to ride the haul road out and back.

Pescadero Road has a two-mile climb up Haskins Hill, followed by a one-mile descent to Alpine Road. You'll have four miles of uphill riding before descending to Portola State Park. Once inside the park, ride past the campgrounds and pick up the service road. Cross Pescadero Creek on a wooden bridge, immediately turn right, and walk your bike a short distance on a narrow trail,

Old Haul Road in Pescadero Creek Park has easy railroad gradients. Logging by train ended in the 1950s.

12.0 Ride around gate on "Service Area" road.

12.6 Bridge over Pescadero Creek. Take immediate right on narrow trail. Walk bike.

12.7 Iverson Cabin. Ride west up steep road.

12.8 Right on Old Haul Road at gate.

13.9 Bridge Trail junction. Keep left.

16.7 Left at junction. Crucial intersection.

17.6 Ride around gate. Keep left.

17.7 Keep right at junction.

18.1 Ride ends.

■

which will lead you to the Iverson cabin. Christian Iverson, a Scandinavian immigrant who worked as a pony express rider and armed guard, built the cabin in the 1860s. Continue on the old road, which crosses Pescadero Creek and goes up to the Old Haul Road. Turn right at the gate.

Take the Bridge Trail if you want to see Pescadero Creek, nestled in the redwoods and lined with willows. The creek supports an abundance of life, including steelhead trout, crawfish, kingfisher, raccoon, opossum, and deer. No fishing or hunting is allowed in the park. The bridge is a Bailey-type and makes a peaceful location to get some sun.

Continue on the haul road and take a left at the next junction. Go straight at the junction past the wire cable. After the ride there's food and drink waiting at the Loma Mar Store a mile-and-a-half west of the trailhead on Pescadero Road. You can take either Wurr Road or Pescadero Road to get there. This is an authentic "country" store with a fireplace, pool table, and TV. Owner Roger Siebecker runs the business seven days a week and also serves as the town postmaster and volunteer fireman. There's no better place to relax than the store's front patio, where you can watch the world go by from deep within the redwoods.

30. Purisima Creek

Distance: **21 miles.**
Terrain: **Hilly.**
Traffic: **Hikers, equestrians, bicyclists.**

In the late 1800s logging had shifted from the readily accessible eastern ridges to the more remote coastal canyons of the Santa Cruz Mountains. Dozens of roads were made for dragging logs by oxen to nearby mills. The logs were shipped from the mill by horse and wagon to the port of Redwood City. Some of the roads have survived and, although paved, remain mostly unchanged.

Purisima Creek Road is one of those early logging roads, and you can explore it by bicycle in a park setting. Now a dedicated trail, the four-mile dirt road is used by hikers, equestrians, and bicyclists. The tranquil beauty of the lower canyon includes redwood groves, fern-draped canyon walls, and burbling Purisima Creek.

Your ride begins at a Midpeninsula Regional Open Space District parking lot on Skyline Boulevard, 2.4 miles north of Kings Mountain Road. You'll take the steep Harkins Fire Trail to the bottom of Purisima Canyon, ride west to the coast on Higgins Purisima Road, turn south on Highway 1, and finish by riding up Purisima Canyon.

Harkins Fire Trail offers gorgeous views of the ocean and brush-covered ridges. Early in the ride you'll skirt the upper reaches of Whittemore Gulch on a narrow trail on the way to Harkins Fire Trail. Ride carefully and watch for other trail users.

On foggy summer days the coast may be smothered in a blanket of white fog. It can be hot on Skyline but damp and cool in the canyon.

After crossing Purisima Creek on a wooden

Mileage Log

0.0 Start mileage at the Midpeninsula Regional Open Space District parking lot on Skyline Boulevard, 2.4 miles north of Kings Mountain Road in San Mateo County. Leave parking lot headed west on old logging road.

0.3 Left on hiking trail.

0.9 Right on Harkins Fire Trail.

3.4 Cross Purisima Creek bridge. Right on Purisima Creek Road.

3.5 Exit parking lot, go right, and climb Higgins Purisima Road.

▼

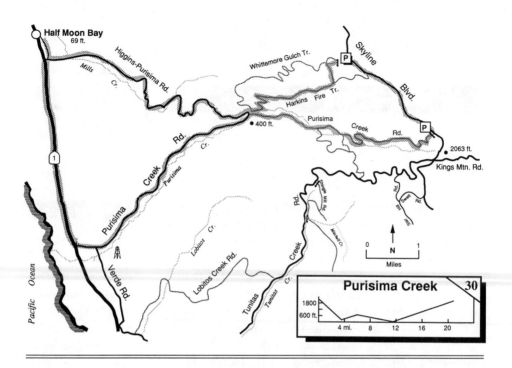

Purisima Creek ... 30

1800
600 ft.
4 mi.   8   12   16   20

7.8 Left on Highway 1 at stop sign.

To reach Ocean Shore Railroad station: 0.0 Right on Main Street. 0.4 Left on Poplar Street. 1.1 Left on Railroad Avenue (building on right). 1.2 Left on Grove Street. 1.6 Right on Highway 1. 9.0 Restaurant on right.

11.0 Left on Verde Road.

11.3 Purisima town site on left.

▼

bridge, you'll leave the park on Purisima Creek Trail through a parking area at Higgins Purisima Road. The road was paved for the first time in 1987. Turn right and climb for a half-mile before descending to Highway 1. Vegetable fields line the coast. On the left you'll see the white-frame Johnston house, built in 1853 by James Johnston, who made his fortune as a land speculator and saloon keeper in San Francisco. Johnston and his three brothers built the first road from the bayside to the coast through Pilarcitos Valley, just north of Highway 92.

Half Moon Bay is only a mile to the north, reached by turning right on Main Street at the Highway 1 intersection. There's a bakery, a well-stocked general store, and a bike shop downtown on Main Street. An interesting building west of town is the former Ocean Shore Railroad station on Railroad Avenue (see Mileage Log). The Ocean Shore Railroad was established in 1905 by land speculators who hoped to develop the coast from San Francisco to Santa Cruz. But the railroad failed to catch on, reaching only as far as Tunitas Creek, and shut down in 1920.

Ride south on Highway 1 to the junction of Purisima Creek Road, the site of Purisima, a thriving community at the turn of the century. All that remains today is a grove of cypress. As you pass Verde Road look for an old oil derrick to the right on the far hillside. This was the first oil well in San Mateo County in 1867. The well had produced 41,000 barrels when it was abandoned in 1948. Farther up the canyon horses graze next to small oil wells in the front yards of ranch houses.

Return to Purisima Canyon at the car lot and begin climbing Purisima Creek Trail. The gradient varies from flat to 8 and 12 percent. After a left hairpin the climb gets steeper as redwoods give way to dense chaparral, tan oak, and bay laurel. Rufus Hatch and George Borden started logging the canyon in the 1850s; a saw mill in the lower canyon was operated until the early 1920s.

11.4 Keep straight at Verde Road junction on Purisima Creek Road.

12.5 Oil well on right in field.

14.9 Gate to Purisima Creek Road. Begin climb to Skyline.

16.3 Grabtown Gulch Trail on right. Goes to Tunitas Creek Road.

19.2 Skyline Boulevard. Go left.

19.5 Richards Road trail on right.

19.8 Snack bar.

21.2 Return to start at parking lot.

■

Distance: **21 miles.**
Terrain: **Hilly.**
Traffic: **Light traffic,
hikers, bicyclists,
equestrians.**

31. Stevens Canyon

Mileage Log

0.0 Start mileage at Stevens Creek Park from first signed parking lot to left on Stevens Canyon Road. Ride up steep hill for 25 yards and turn left on Stevens Canyon Road.

0.7 Stevens Canyon Dam.

1.2 Right on Montebello Road.

1.7 Picchetti Ranch and Sunrise Winery.

2.6 Jimsomare vineyard.

5.6 Ridge Winery on left.

6.4 Locked gate. Continue north on paved road, which soon turns to dirt.

8.0 Black Mountain summit with microwave towers.

8.2 Gate.

▼

Stevens Canyon, about 10 miles west of Santa Clara Valley, is one of the nearest and most accessible trail rides for local cyclists. A trail through the canyon lies directly on the San Andreas Fault and follows an old "skid road" made for hauling redwood and Douglas fir by ox teams in the late 1800s . More recently the road was used by farmers and ranchers to service orchards on the surrounding ridges. Today the canyon and ridges are public open space.

This tour starts in Stevens Creek Park a few miles west of Cupertino at the site of an old ranch and the Villa Maria winery, used by the University of Santa Clara between 1872 and 1944. The first settler to the area was Captain Elisha Stephens in 1850. Park headquarters, down the hill from the parking lot, houses a small museum.

The ride follows Stevens Creek Reservoir, an earthen dam built in 1936. After a brief warm up on level ground you'll begin a long climb on Montebello Road, with gradients as steep as 15 percent. Two wineries are located on this road, Picchetti and Ridge. The Picchetti property is leased by Sunrise Winery in Boulder Creek from the Open Space District. The public agency maintains the ranch and winery, which was built in the 1870s. The historic site includes a wine cellar and old wine equipment. Wine tastings are held Friday, Saturday, and Sunday from 11 a.m. to 3 p.m.

Ridge Winery, situated in an old ranch house overlooking Santa Clara Valley high up on Monte-

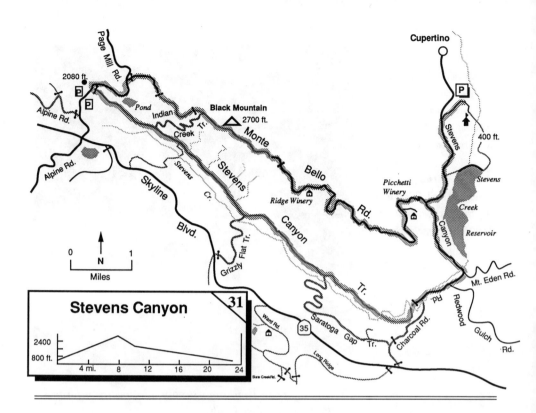

Stevens Canyon

31

bello Ridge, is open Saturdays for wine tasting. Established in the late 1800s and revived in 1962 after a lengthy shutdown, the winery was purchased from its Palo Alto owners by Japanese investors in 1987.

It's another mile from Ridge Winery to a locked gate. The pavement ends about a quarter-mile past the gate. The final climb to Black Mountain summit takes you over an exposed ridge, from which you'll have views of valleys on both sides. At the top you can see San Francisco and the San Andreas Fault. If you want to cut the ride short, you can descend Indian Creek Trail to Stevens Canyon. Take the first left on a ranch road as you descend from the top of Black Mountain. You'll find the trailhead sign about .3 miles down the road next to an occupied ranch. Indian Creek Trail is a wide, steep road.

For the complete ride continue north to Page

8.5 Right at junction. Go left at junction for .1 miles if you want water from a spigot at the backpack camp.

9.5 Locked gate.

10.0 Left on Page Mill Road at gate.

10.5 Left at entrance to signed Stevens Canyon Trail.

11.7 Right at Indian Creek Trail junction.

▼

13.6 Straight at Grizzly Flat Trail junction. Santa Clara County sign says bicyclists must wear helmets on rest of trail. Trail enters Stevens Creek County Park here.

13.9 Left up unmarked trail. This is a new trail section, built by ROMP mountain bike club.

14.4 Ford Stevens Creek.

14.7 Wooden barrier.

14.8 Stevens Canyon Road begins.

15.1 Cross Stevens Creek pouring over road.

17.2 Redwood Gulch Road intersection.

18.8 Left at stop sign. Pierce Road on right.

21.4 End of ride at parking lot.

■

Stevens Canyon Trail drops steeply into a canyon formed by the San Andreas Fault.

Mill Road and take a left. Stevens Canyon Trail joins Page Mill at a dip in the road on the left. You'll descend 1,200 feet in the next five miles, through meadows of golden wild oats in the summer, followed by oaks, buckeyes, tan oaks, and finally redwoods and Douglas firs deep in the damp, dark canyon.

Stevens Canyon lies directly over the San Andreas Fault. Telltale sinkholes and distorted earth can be seen 200 yards after picking up Stevens Canyon Trail at Page Mill Road. On the left, in a thicket of willows, there's a sag pond covered with lilies. Bedrock below the fault has been reduced to clay by the earth's movements, forcing groundwater to the surface. When parts of this hillside sank, they formed a barrier against which groundwater was trapped; sediment will eventually fill the shallow pond.

The trail descends steadily with a couple of short, steep climbs in the first two miles. Keep your speed down and watch for other trail users, including tarantulas slowly crossing the trail in the fall.

Deep in the canyon you'll come to a circular clearing where there's a trail sign for Saratoga Gap on the right. You'll take the unmarked, narrow trail on the left going uphill. Watch out for poison oak; it grows over the trail in the spring. After a short, steep descent, you'll ford Stevens Creek and cross a major landslide on a narrow bench. Cross Stevens Creek once again (it spills over the paved road) and you're back on pavement. It's mostly downhill to Stevens Creek Reservoir. Stevens Canyon can be enjoyed year round, but it's especially nice on hot days or in the fall when the leaves are turning.

32. Tilden-Wildcat Parks

Mileage Log

0.0 Start mileage in Tilden Park at Lone Oak picnic area (drinking fountain) off Central Park Drive. Ride south on Sweetbriar Canyon Trail, uphill.

1.4 Right, downhill, on Curran Trail.

2.0 Right on Wildcat Gorge Trail, downhill.

2.8 Return to Lone Oak picnic area. Begin riding right and north on pavement, which becomes Loop Trail.

3.0 Gate.

3.9 Jewel Lake on left.

4.6 Gate. Entering Wildcat Park.

▼

Tilden and Wildcat parks provide a protected environment for plants, animals, and East Bay mountain bike riders seeking refuge from auto traffic. These parks are the last parcels of open space in the East Bay hills. Berkeley and Oakland residents can ride out their back doors to enjoy scenic areas in relative isolation. On weekdays the parks are lightly used, especially the remote interior of Wildcat Park.

Off-road bike riding in the East Bay regional parks is carefully monitored by park rangers. The Berkeley/East Bay Bicycle Trails Council is also diligently working to inform bicyclists about safe riding and to keep roads open. Cyclists may ride on most fire and service roads in the parks but are not permitted on any narrow hiking trails. The map shows only those trails open to bicycles.

This tour begins in Tilden Park with a short loop that includes a long climb and descent. It's followed by a much larger loop through Wildcat Park, where you'll climb to the park's highest point and return on the paved Nimitz Way.

Begin riding on Sweetbriar Canyon Trail up a grassy hillside to Curran Trail, which takes you into a narrow canyon through eucalyptus and redwoods. Look for caves on the west canyon wall. Turn right and take Wildcat Gorge Trail through riparian habitat, kept moist by springs year round. Willows grow close to the trail. To reduce trail damage, this trail is open only in the dry season.

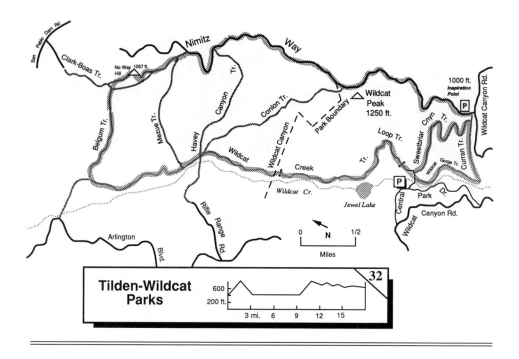

Tilden-Wildcat Parks

Back at the Lone Oak picnic area where you started, ride north on a paved road that soon turns to dirt beyond a gate that marks the Loop Trail. The wide dirt road takes you through a dense eucalyptus forest and into Wildcat Canyon. Jewel Lake on the left is part of the Tilden Nature Area, where bicycles are allowed only on Loop Trail. Biologists involved in a nature study program use the 740-acre parcel year round.

In Wildcat Park you'll see hillsides covered with thistle, identified by their spectacular purple and red flowers and large seed pods. There's an eerie feeling here that evokes images of *Invasion of the Body Snatchers*, a science fiction thriller in which giant pod-like plants containing aliens are sent to Earth to "occupy" human bodies. In fact, there is a serious invasion taking place here: Thistles, which flourish where land has been overgrazed, have become entrenched in the area. They're difficult to eradicate and they spread quickly.

5.9 Trail junction for Havey Canyon, Conlon, and Rifle Range Road trails. Go straight.

6.9 Old parking lot.

7.6 Right on Belgum Trail, uphill. Gate at 8.0.

8.6 Keep left at Y-intersection. Bottom of hill at 8.7. Begin climb-walk up No Way Hill.

8.8 Summit.

9.3 Second Summit.

▼

Loop Trail in Tilden Park near Jewel Lake passes through a eucalyptus grove.

9.8 Mezue Trail junction. Keep left around corral.

10.1 Gate.

10.2 Begin paved Nimitz Way.

11.9 Ckonlon Trail on right.

14.2 Inspiration Point. Right on Curran Trail, then right again on Sweetbriar Canyon.

15.7 Ride ends at Lone Oak picnic area.

∎

Next you'll ride across an old parking lot that washed out during the winter floods of 1982–83. In less than a mile turn right on Belgum Trail, where there's a steep climb to Clark Boas Trail through more thistle and a palm grove where a house once stood.

Keep left at the Clark-Boas junction and ride around "No Way Hill" to the north face, where you'll find a steep dirt road that goes straight up. It's followed by another steep climb to a knoll. Your reward is a clear view of the park and San Francisco, San Pablo, and Suisun bays.

San Pablo Ridge Trail joins Nimitz Way, where you'll see concrete missile silos that were abandoned in the 1960s. Nimitz Way hugs a ridgetop extending to Inspiration Point. Take Curran Trail on the right in the parking lot, ride down the hill, go right at Sweetbriar Canyon Trail, and return to your start at the Lone Oak picnic area.

Tilden Park was named in honor of Major Charles Lee Tilden, a park founder and first presi-

Use low gears when climbing the summit following No Way Hill in Wildcat Canyon Park.

dent of the park district's board of directors. It is one of three original regional parks established in 1936. The others are the Robert Sibley Volcanic Regional Preserve and the Temescal Regional Recreation Area.

III. Casual Rides

33. San Leandro Bay

Distance: **5 miles.**
Terrain: **Flat.**
Traffic: **Pedestrians, bicyclists.**

While San Leandro Bay lacks quiet solitude, its 1,218-acre nature preserve is a lovely environment for biking in. Only 77 acres of wetlands remain compared to the more than 2,000 acres that existed as late as 1915. However, it's a start at preserving this important wildlife habitat.

Located between the Nimitz Freeway and Oakland Airport, San Leandro Bay Regional Shoreline offers hiking, bicycling, birding, fishing, sunbathing, and boating. It's easily accessible by BART from either Hegenberger Road or 66th Avenue.

A fishing pier is located on Doolittle Drive, next to a boat launch, and there's Doolittle Beach farther north. A bike lane runs the entire length of Doolittle Drive.

The recreation path extends several miles around the bay, passing warehouses and an open, graded field. Watch for pedestrians strolling along the path and keep your speed below 15 mph; besides pedestrians, you might run over ground squirrels that dart across.

Arrowhead Marsh and San Leandro Creek are the best places for birding. Shorebirds are most commonly seen at low tide, poking around in the mud looking for food. Among the birds you'll see are egrets, great blue herons, avocets, long-billed curlews, willets, and a variety of sandpipers.

In 1882 San Leandro Bay was the scene of a tragic train accident. At the turn of the century the bay was a large marsh extending inland past San Leandro Boulevard and west over most of what is

Mileage Log

0.0 Start mileage at Visitor Center, San Leandro Bay Regional Shoreline, about a mile north at end of dirt road off Swan Way. Ride south on San Leandro Creek Trail.

0.9 Ride over San Leandro Creek on Hegenberger Road bridge.

1.9 **Left on bridge over Elmhurst Creek.**

2.6 Garetson Point. Restrooms and water. Turn around and retrace path. At Visitor Center continue on path headed west. Turn around at parking area next to Swan Way and return to Visitor Center.

5.2 End of ride.
■

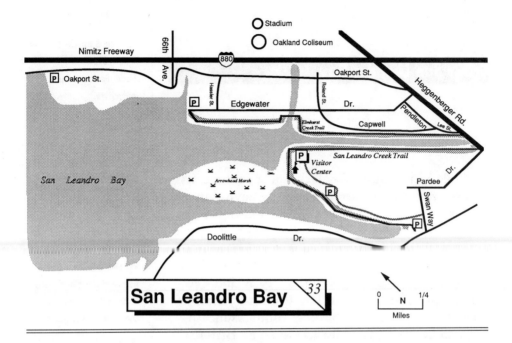

San Leandro Bay 33

Stadium

Oakland Coliseum

Nimitz Freeway

66th Ave.

880

Oakport St.

Oakport St.

Hassler St.

Edgewater

Roland St.

Dr.

Heggenberger Rd.

Pendleton

Lee St.

Elmhurst Creek Trail

Capwell

San Leandro Creek Trail

Visitor Center

Dr.

San Leandro Bay

Arrowhead Marsh

Pardee

Swan Way

Doolittle

Dr.

0 N 1/4

Miles

now Oakland Airport. Train tracks ran just to the
west of Doolittle Drive, but they were constantly
sinking into the mud.

On the evening of September 11, a northbound
South Pacific Coast freight train hit a bad section
of track and pitched over on its side into the bay
mud. Fireman Dan Driscoll was pinned under the
locomotive. In a scene reminiscent of Ken Kesey's
novel *Sometimes a Great Notion*, the train crew
worked frantically against the rising tide to free
him, but to no avail.

The bridge was damaged and dismantled shortly
after the 1906 earthquake. Now there's a vehicle
bridge where the train bridge stood. Trains carrying passengers between Oakland and Santa Cruz
have long since quit running, and the marshy
waters where the trainman died are now airport
runways.

34. Hellyer Park

Distance: **13 miles.**
Terrain: **Flat.**
Traffic: **Pedestrians, bicyclists.**

Coyote Creek and the 223-acre Hellyer Park offer an ideal setting for a casual family outing and bike ride. This tour starts from the Hellyer Park Velodrome, Northern California's only bicycle racing track. Built in 1962, the 336-meter concrete oval is owned by Santa Clara County. Ed Steffani, a retired civil engineer from Los Gatos, designed and helped build the track.

On Friday nights in the summer you can catch a race under the lights. As many as 1,000 spectators fill the bleachers to watch furious sprints and adroit bike handling. On weekends you might see riders training in the late afternoon or morning. San Jose was a hotbed for track racing in the 1920s and '30s, when gambling on races was a popular pastime.

Start riding along the bike path on the right side of the parking lot entrance. You'll follow Coyote Creek for 12 miles out and back, often under the shade of cottonwoods, sycamores, and stately oaks. San Jose and Santa Clara County retain a public right-of-way along most of the creek's 31 miles. About seven miles of new path was added in 1991, extending south from Metcalf Road to Morgan Hill in Coyote Creek Park. The Coyote Creek Park pedestrian/bike path is maintained by Santa Clara County.

The path dips under the Hellyer Avenue bridge and then passes Cottonwood Lake on the left. The lake is stocked with trout and bluegill. There are picnic tables and barbecues as well as a playground

Mileage Log

0.0 Hellyer Park Velodrome, San Jose. Take bike path on right side of parking lot, following Coyote Creek.

0.6 Cottonwood Lake.

2.4 Bridge on right takes you to a residential park and playground.

3.1 Right turn on Piercy Road, cross bridge and immediately turn left.

4.7 Cross Tenant Avenue.

5.8 Ride under Highway 101.

6.0 Path turns to dirt. Weir on left.

6.6 Parkway Lakes County Park on left. Return same route.

▼

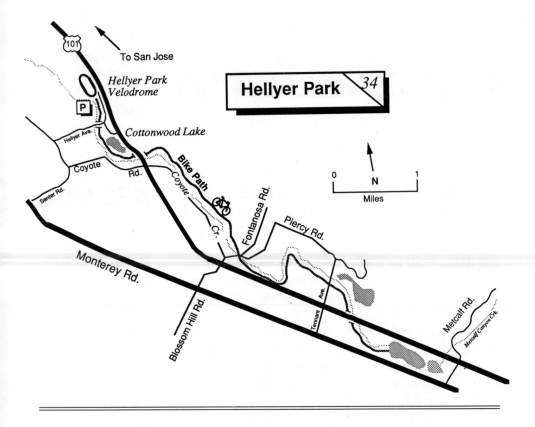

13.2 End of ride.

■

nearby where you can take the kids. The eight-foot-wide trail heads down a gentle incline under Highway 101. The normally placid creek flooded in the early 1980s, wiping out a section of the trail. Unfortunately, close to Hellyer Avenue the creek is polluted with such debris as tires and wrecked cars.

Although the trail nears a few industrial parks, it isn't difficult to imagine the way Santa Clara Valley must have been 40 years ago when it was mostly an agricultural valley.

At 3.1 miles cross Piercy Road Bridge, turn right, and then take an immediate left. Watch for cars as you make your turn. The trail picks up on the west side of the creek, winding through orchards and past farm houses.

The bike track, called a velodrome, at Hellyer Park is the scene of weekend racing and training.

At 5.8 miles you'll pass under a new section of Highway 101, where you'll find blackberry bushes growing in abundance along the creek. The paved trail ends a short distance from here at a weir. The route becomes a rocky dirt trail if you continue south. To the west is Monterey Highway, which used to be Highway 101 before the new highway was built.

South of Metcalf Road the trail has two paved sections, each about .8 miles in length; the trail ends at a farm house in the middle of a junk yard, however.

Return on the same path. Coyote Creek is a good place to stay cool on a hot day. In the spring when the winds are blowing you can seek shelter among the trees.

Hellyer Park's bike path winds through orchards bordering Coyote Creek.

35. Coyote Hills Park

Distance: **3 or 21 miles.**
Terrain: **Flat.**
Traffic: **Pedestrians, equestrians, bicyclists.**

Imagine 14 miles of recreation path with sweeping views of San Francisco Bay and you'll start to have a sense of what Coyote Hills Park is like. From a bench overlooking the bay you can watch sunsets or the moon rise. You'll also see deer, bobcats, and other wildlife, all in a natural setting, at this park that's located near the eastern approach to Dumbarton Bridge.

After exploring the park by bicycle you'll understand why the Ohlone Indians settled here. Enormous shell mounds bear witness to the fruitful bounty they found in Alameda Creek and the bay. Reeds from the marsh were used to make boats, baskets, and huts. The hills provided abundant rock suitable for fashioning arrowheads. Ohlone culture and artifacts are on display at park headquarters or you can tour the marshes on your own.

There's a rolling 3.5-mile paved path around the base of the hills in the 1,021-acre park. From the eastern side you're riding next to the bay, with views of San Jose, the Santa Cruz Mountains, and San Francisco.

For a longer ride follow Alameda Creek Trail on a bike path that passes under all road and train crossings. The Army Corps of Engineers built the trail as part of a flood control project in 1973. Stay on the south side of the creek going both directions. The north side is designated for horseback riding. You'll see many egrets, great blue herons, and ducks along the creek.

Mileage Log

0.0 Mileage starts at the Visitor Center in Coyote Hills Regional Park. Ride southeast toward Patterson Ranch Road.

0.3 Right at parking lot and path, where you'll see restrooms and a picnic area. Stay on paved path at all times for this loop.

1.0 Right at junction. Apay Way on left. It's 1.6 miles from here to Highway 84 and the National Wildlife Refuge.

2.6 Left at junction to reach Alameda Creek Trail to Niles Canyon. Keep right to return to visitor center.

▼

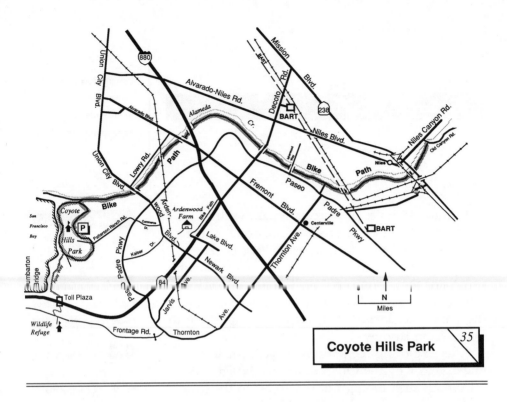

3.4 Visitor center.

■

**Ride from Visitor Center
to Niles Canyon on
Alameda Creek Trail.**

0.0 Start at Visitor Center
and ride toward bay on
Bayview Trail.

0.8 Right at junction
to reach Alameda Creek
Trail. Right on Alameda
Creek path. For side trip
to Ardenwood Historic
Farm, turn left on
Ardenwood Boulevard.

▼

Ardenwood Historic Farm, 1.5 miles east of Coyote Hills, is an interesting side trip. You can get there from the trail by riding up the exit road (Ardenwood Boulevard) at the first bridge. It's about a mile to the park entrance on the left. Ardenwood has been preserved to recreate a 19th century farm: The land is tilled by horse and plow, cows are milked by hand, and the house—built in 1883—has furniture of the period. You can tour on foot or go by horse-drawn flat car on railroad tracks. The farm is closed between November 15 and April 1, although it opens for a few days around Christmas. Admission is $4 on weekends, less on weekdays. For more information write or call Ardenwood Historic Farm, 34600 Ardenwood Boulevard, Fremont 94555; (415) 796-0663.

Six miles from Coyote Hills you'll ride under Interstate 880 and then turn south. Near the end of the path you'll see rock quarries and railroad yards.

In the Niles District (just south of the path) during World War I Charlie Chaplin made five of his early movies with Gloria Swanson. Essanay Studios moved to Hollywood in 1916.

By taking Apay Way, a dirt road in Coyote Hills Park, you can also visit the National Wildlife Refuge south of Dumbarton Bridge. Dense brush and dill growing along the road provide cover for deer and bobcats. You'll cross Highway 84 on a pedestrian bridge. Cyclists coming from the peninsula can take a recreation path over Dumbarton Bridge and continue east on the frontage road. Riding over the 1.6-mile span offers a unique view of San Francisco Bay. Guided tours of the refuge are offered by bike and on foot. For more information call (415) 792-0222.

2.5 Union City Boulevard.

3.2 Train tracks.

3.9 Alvarado Boulevard.

4.1 Interstate 880.

5.8 Decoto Road.

6.6 Isherwood Way.

9.3 BART and train tracks.

10.3 Mission Boulevard.

10.5 Old Canyon Road Bridge. End of trail. Return by same route.

21.0 End of ride.

■

36. San Mateo and Foster City Bike Paths

Mileage Log

0.0 Start mileage at Coyote Point Park, San Mateo, in the Eucalyptus Group Picnic area behind the museum and next to Coyote Point Yacht Harbor. Ride south through the parking lot.

0.1 Gerry Mon Memorial Bike Path, dedicated by the city of San Mateo in 1987.

1.2 Cross San Mateo Creek. Watch for narrow barriers.

2.1 Cross the old East Third Avenue Bridge over Marina Lagoon to Foster City.

4.0 Ride under Highway 92. The fishing pier parking lot is on the south side. Path continues south and west along Belmont Slough, then north along Marina Lagoon.

▼

Foster City has miles of level, paved paths along San Francisco Bay. They're ideal for bicycling if you're willing to put up with a little wind, as it's almost always breezy on the bay.

Bicycling on this recreation path between San Mateo and Foster City offers a tantalizing preview of what the "Ring Around the Bay" might look like when it's finally completed. This path and others are part of a 250-mile bay trail proposed by Senator Bill Lockyer.

Although the complete trail is still years away, you can tour a 10-mile section named for the late Gerry Mon, a San Mateo engineer who was instrumental in having the trail built with federal and state transportation funds.

The ride starts at Coyote Point Park in San Mateo. The park, located on a rocky knoll with a dense eucalyptus grove, has a long history as a recreation site. In 1922 Pacific City Amusement Park opened here to huge crowds. It was modeled on New York's Coney Island, and visitors could ride a roller coaster, do the tango in a large dance hall, swim in the bay, sunbathe on a sandy beach, or dine in fine restaurants. The multi-million dollar project lasted only two years, however, as the initial excitement soon wore off and attendance dropped. A fire destroyed one-quarter of the grounds and raw sewage in the bay closed the beach.

Today's park has a clean, sandy beach, the bay water isn't too polluted, and you can still find a

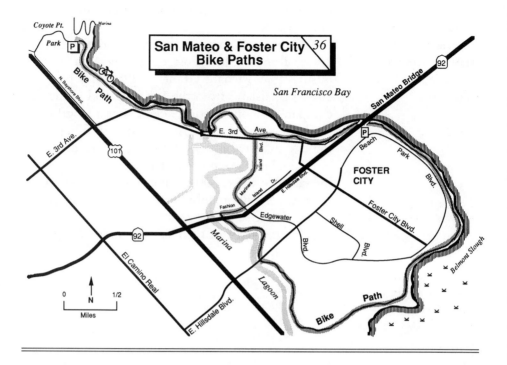

San Mateo & Foster City
Bike Paths \36

Coyote Pt.
Park

Marina

San Francisco Bay

San Mateo Bridge 92

Bike Path

N. Bayshore Blvd

E. 3rd Ave.

101

E. 3rd Ave.

Island Blvd.

Mariners Island Dr.

E. Hillsdale Blvd

Beach

Park

FOSTER CITY

Blvd.

Foster City Blvd.

Belmont Slough

92

El Camino Real

Fashion

Edgewater

Shell Blvd

Blvd

Blvd.

Marina Lagoon

Bike Path

0   1/2

N

Miles

E. Hillsdale Blvd.

fancy restaurant (The Castaways) with a view of jets landing at San Francisco airport. There's also an excellent interpretive museum, a golf course, and a marina.

The bike path starts from the Marina at the back of the park and extends south to Foster City and Belmont Slough. You can ride at least nine miles one way along the bay, almost all the way around Foster City. A major challenge to completing the path was the old, narrow East Avenue bridge over Marina Lagoon. A new bridge was finished in 1987; the old bridge was saved for pedestrians and bicyclists.

As you ride south (winds are usually out of the north) you'll go under the massive steel towers of San Mateo Bridge. South of the bridge in Foster City you're riding on landfill. Foster City is built around Brewer Island. At the turn of the century nearby wetlands were converted to salt ponds. The levees you're riding on were built to keep out the

9.9 Ride under East Hillsdale Boulevard overpass and keep left.

10.9 Ride under Highway 92 overpass, then take first right on sidewalk into parking lot. Exit parking lot onto Fashion Island Boulevard. Take right turn from parking lot.

11.1 Left at stoplight in Mariner's Island Park.

▼

12.1 **Left on Third Street at stoplight. Right onto recreation path, continuing north back to start.**

14.3 End of ride.
■

bay water; without them Foster City would be under water.

This planned community was the dream of Texas oil man T. Jack Foster and Bay Area businessman Richard Grant. In 1959 they purchased the island from the Schilling and Leslie Salt companies. Construction began after a lengthy battle by environmentalists opposed to filling in the bay. A state bill was drawn up to create a municipal improvement district that would govern the city. By 1964, 200 families lived in Foster City. At least 18 million cubic yards of fill was used. Today Foster City has 28,000 residents.

A circular tour of the city is included in the Mileage Log.

37. Lake Chabot

Distance: **6 or 11 miles.**
Terrain: **Rolling hills.**
Traffic: **Pedestrians, bicyclists.**

Anthony Chabot Regional Park and Lake Chabot offer a secluded setting in a canyon above Castro Valley. Recreational opportunities besides bicycling include fishing, boating, camping, birding, and hiking. Boats can be rented at the Marina, but no private boats or swimming are allowed.

Among the birds you'll see are geese and ducks feeding next to the marina and in the 512-acre lake. Listen carefully and you'll hear the distinctive song of two prominent birds in the park. The olive-sided flycatcher perches on tree tops and has a song like "Mc-Min-Ville." The wren tit is found in chaparral; its trilling call resembles the sound of a bouncing ping-pong ball, starting out slowly and then picking up speed.

If you ride to the east end of the lake, you can either visit an extensive marsh along San Leandro Creek or ride west and tour the dam. Use caution on the narrow paths and watch your speed on the downhills. Get an early start to avoid the crowds.

The 4,674-acre park has miles of hiking trails and most fire roads are open to bicycles. There's also an equestrian center, marksmanship range, and youth group camping.

The park is named for Anthony Chabot, who built the earthen dam and created the Contra Costa Water Company in 1866. The dam was completed in 1874 by 800 laborers with teams of horses to move and compact the soil. The park was originally named Grass Valley Regional Park, after a nearby ranch of the same name. Most of the

Mileage Log

0.0 Start at the Marina and ride north on the West Shore Trail.

1.5 Lake Chabot Dam.

3.0 Return to Marina.

3.1 Ride around grass field on path and cross footbridge. Right turn on East Shore Trail.

4.6 Turn around at end of pavement.

6.3 Return to Marina.

The mileage for a complete loop of the park follows. For experienced mountain bike riders only. Pick up mileage from Lake Chabot Dam.

■

▼

1.5 Lake Chabot Dam. Cross dam and ride uphill on paved service road. Bass Cove Trail has several forks on knoll overlooking dam. Stay on middle trail heading east.

2.7 Left at junction, uphill. Bass Cove Trail goes steeply downhill to lake. Closed to bicycles.

3.0 Begin Goldenrod Trail and steady climb. Keep right at junction.

3.1 Right on a paved golf course path.

3.2 Right on dirt road. Trail parallels housing on left.

4.1 Right on Jackson Grade, downhill.

4.5 Keep right after crossing stone bridge on Brandon Trail.

5.8 Right at junction.

5.9 View of Oakland and San Francisco.

6.8 Right at junction, staying on Brandon Trail. Do not take Logger's Loop on right.

parkland was consolidated into watershed for the city of Oakland in the early 1900s. The eucalyptus trees were planted in 1910.

7.6 Cross paved Marciel Road and continue south on Brandon Trail.

7.8 Right at junction, downhill on unsigned Thistle Hill Trail.

8.0 Left at junction after circling hill and leveling out, with Marciel Road on right. Begin steep downhill on Live Oak Trail.

8.6 Right at bottom of hill.

8.7 Left on narrow trail in trees. Cross foot bridge over marsh.

8.8 Right on Cameron Loop Trail.

8.9 Pick up paved East Shore Trail along lake.

10.6 End of ride at Lake Chabot Marina.

■

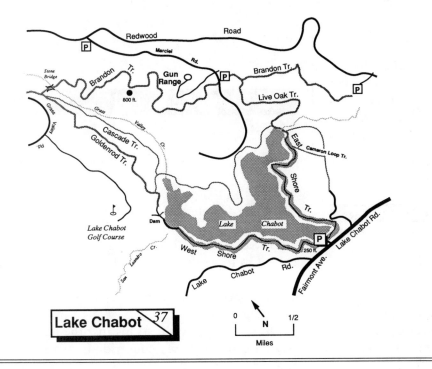

Redwood Road

Marciel Rd.

Brandon Tr.

Gun Range

Brandon Tr.

Live Oak Tr.

Stone Bridge

Brandon Tr.

800 ft.

Grass Valley

Cascade Tr.

Goldenrod Tr.

Cr.

East Shore Tr.

Cameron Loop Tr.

Lake Chabot Golf Course

Dam

Lake   Chabot

West Shore Tr.

250 ft.

Lake Chabot Rd.

Fairmont Ave.

San Leandro Cr.

Lake   Chabot   Rd.

Lake Chabot *37*

0   **N**   1/2

Miles

Distance: **11 miles.**
Terrain: **One moderate hill.**
Traffic: **Hikers, joggers, bicyclists.**

38. Sawyer Camp Trail

Mileage Log

0.0 Start mileage at south access on Sawyer Camp Trail at the Skyline Boulevard and Crystal Springs Road intersection near Hillsborough. Limited parking available here. Ride north.

3.4 Water, toilets, picnic tables. Historic bay tree located 25 yards to west of tables.

5.0 Top of San Andreas Dam.

5.9 North entrance to Sawyer Camp Trail at Hillcrest Boulevard. Return same way or you can take frontage road back to Sawyer Camp Trail. Ride up the freeway ramp onto Interstate 280 heading south. Stay on the walkway until ramp ends.

▼

Sawyer Camp Trail is the most popular trail in San Mateo County, running directly over the infamous San Andreas Fault along Crystal Springs Lake. On this ride you probably won't feel an earthquake, but seeing pristine blue reservoirs in Crystal Springs Valley will certainly be a moving experience.

On some Sundays it seems that the hordes of Bay Area residents walking, riding, or running on Sawyer Camp Trail could shake the earth. As many as 1,300 visitors flock to the narrow, paved path along the east shore of Upper Crystal Springs Reservoir on a busy Sunday. About 300,000 people visit the trail annually. Weaving between trees and shrubs, the path's many twists and turns add variety and provide spectacular vistas of the Crystal Springs Valley.

Start your tour at the south entrance, where you'll find portable toilets and a fountain. Riding north on a smooth eight-foot-wide path, you'll see Crystal Springs Reservoir on your left. The peninsula's water supply is closely monitored by the San Francisco Water Department. There's usually a refreshing breeze on the shaded ride among oaks, buckeyes, and tan oaks. At 3.4 miles the trail has restrooms and a drinking fountain. Nearby you'll find picnic tables and, a short distance off the trail, one of the oldest and largest bay laurel trees in the state. The Jepson laurel was named in honor of Willis Jepson, a California botanist.

North of the picnic grounds you'll pass fern-

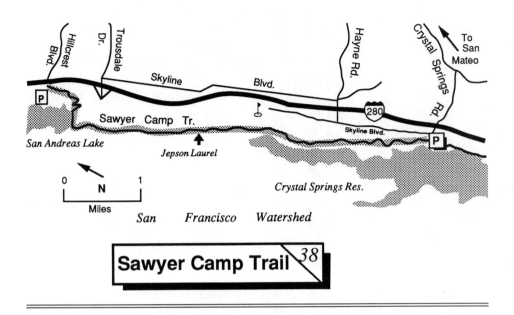

Sawyer Camp Trail ⟍38

covered slopes and a grove of bay trees that provide shade on hot summer days. Springs and a creek keep the area green year round. You'll have a gradual climb to San Andreas Dam, followed by a steeper climb to the north entrance at Hillcrest Boulevard. Retrace the path or, if you're not bothered by cars, return on Skyline Boulevard as described in the Mileage Log.

The best time to ride the trail is at midweek, but if you start early on a weekend, traffic isn't bad once you've ridden a mile from the south entrance, where most people congregate. Obey the posted 10 mph speed limit and always yield to pedestrians.

Sawyer Camp Trail was an isolated dirt road until 1979, when the county paved it and turned it into a dedicated trail. The road's history goes back to the 1850s, when Leander Sawyer kept an inn here to serve picnickers and raise prize circus horses. The valley road later became the main stagecoach route from Millbrae to Half Moon Bay.

Water became a vital issue as San Francisco grew during the gold mining days. San Andreas Reser-

6.6 Take the Trousdale Drive exit. Immediately get on the walkway.

6.7 Left on Trousdale Drive at stop sign.

6.8 Right on Skyline Boulevard at stop sign.

9.7 Right on Golf Course Drive at stop sign.

9.8 Left on Skyline Boulevard at stop sign.

11.1 Return to Sawyer Camp Trail.

∎

voir was built in 1869; in 1934 the Hetch Hetchy pipeline was built to bring water from the Tuolumne River in the High Sierra to San Andreas Lake and its neighboring dams to the south, Upper (1877) and Lower (1888) Crystal Springs Reservoirs. All three dams withstood the 1906 earthquake.

Distance: **10 miles.**
Terrain: **Flat.**
Traffic: **Hikers, bicyclists.**

Shoreline Park is located on the former Mountain View dump, where San Francisco buried its garbage for more than 13 years. Mountain View used its $13 million in dumping fees to pay for the park, which was dedicated in 1983. In addition, methane gas, a byproduct of rotting garbage, is recovered to the tune of $170,000 annually to pay for park maintenance. Today the setting is anything but trashy. The park gained nationwide attention in 1986 with the opening of Bill Graham's elegant Shoreline Ampitheatre, an outdoor concert hall where top recording artists perform.

Most of the park offers a quiet, peaceful setting as you ride on a recreation path winding around the bay. There's an artificially created lake in the center of the park with a boat launch, golf course, and clubhouse.

This tour starts from a parking lot inside the main park entrance at the end of Stierlin Road and loops through Palo Alto baylands out into the bay on dirt levees. As you get started watch for ring-necked pheasant and marsh hawks to the right through a row of pine trees. The path turns west, crosses a wooden bridge over Permanente Creek, and then continues north to a series of salt ponds. At these ponds in the fall and winter you'll find the best duck watching anywhere in the Bay Area.

Follow the path as you pass through an open wooden gate, riding between Coast Casey Forebay on the left and salt ponds on the right. There's a pump house and a portable toilet straight ahead.

Mileage Log

0.0 Start mileage at entrance to Shoreline Park on Shoreline Boulevard. Ride north on recreation path.

1.1 Cross Permanente Creek and take first right. Right again in 50 yards on path. Portable toilets at intersection.

1.7 Right, followed by open wooden gate.

1.9 Right on dirt levee at pump house and portable toilets. Levee heads into bay and returns to Palo Alto.

4.4 Right on road at Palo Alto recycling center. Gate may be closed.

4.6 Straight at Embarcadero Road junction and stop sign.

▼

5.1 Baylands Nature Center on left. Turn around and return by same road.

5.6 Right on Embarcadero Road at stop sign.

6.0 Left on Faber Place next to car dealership.

6.1 Right at end of Faber Place onto recreation path.

6.5 Left at frontage road, staying on recreation path.

8.0 Left on paved path immediately after crossing bridge over Adobe Creek.

8.4 Right at pump house on recreation path.

8.6 Left at T-intersection.

9.2 Left at junction and then left again to cross bridge over Permanente Creek.

10.3 End ride at Shoreline Boulevard park entrance.

■

Turn right at the next junction and ride on a dirt levee that heads out to the bay and goes north to the Palo Alto dump. The Palo Alto dump will be closed and turned into a park within the next decade. Beware: the levee turns to a muddy quagmire in the rain.

After passing the city dump you'll pick up a paved road next to the recycling center. Go around the gate if it's closed and head north to the Baylands Nature Center, beyond Embarcadero Road and the airport. A half-mile north on the left you'll see the center, resting on pilings over the salt marsh. It offers guided bike rides and walks, slide shows, and movies about the bay (415) 329-2506.

Return to Embarcadero Road and turn right. Go .4 miles and turn left onto Faber Place. Pick up the recreation path at the end of the street and head south. You'll cross Matadero Creek, Dry Creek, and then Adobe Creek before turning left to take the path back to the pump station. A path that goes under Highway 101 next to Adobe Creek is open during the dry season. Turn right at the pump house and retrace your route.

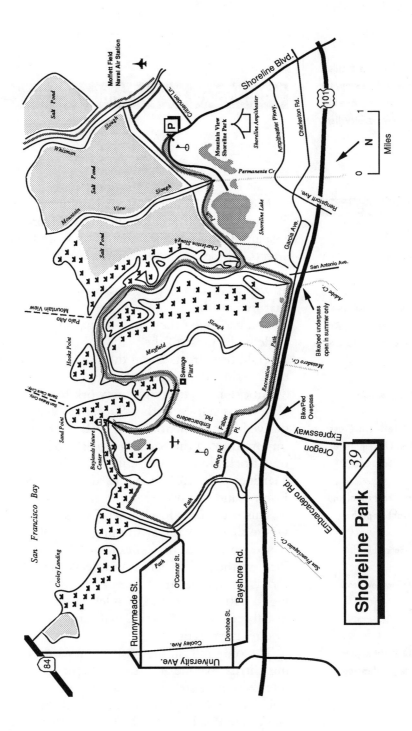

Distance: **8 miles.**
Terrain: **Flat except for**
one hill.
Traffic: **Hikers, bicyclists.**

40. Walnut Creek Canals

Mileage Log

0.0 Start mileage at
Marchbanks Drive on path
across the parking lot from
golf course, in Walnut Creek's
Heather Farms City Park. Ride
north on path along Ygnacio
Canal.

0.2 Lake on right.

0.3 **Left turn. Cross**
road and take path to
Contra Costa Canal.

0.4 **Cross canal and**
turn right on path.

0.8 Bancroft Road.

2.0 Oak Grove Road.

2.7 Citrus Avenue.

2.8 **Right at junc-**
tion. Begin climbing.
▼

More than 15 miles of canals winding through Walnut Creek, Pleasant Hill, and Concord offer casual, mostly flat bike rides away from busy streets. These concrete irrigation canals are visited by a wide variety of ducks in the spring and fall, as well as raccoons, possums, and other wildlife that live nearby.

You can enjoy the canals on paved eight-foot-wide paths most of the way. Although you'll cross several busy streets along the way, you're mostly in quiet residential neighborhoods.

An extensive irrigation network for San Ramon Valley was started in the 1930s, but World War II delayed its completion until 1952. Water is imported from the Sacramento/San Joaquin Delta near Rock Slough, where it eventually winds up in Martinez to be treated and used as drinking water. Fishing and swimming in the canal are prohibited.

This tour starts in Heather Farms City Park, where there's a large swimming pool, playground, concession stand, baseball diamond, and a lake. Pick up the path where it intersects Marchbanks Drive, across the street from the golf course parking lot. Ride north and turn left at the parking lot. You'll see Contra Costa Canal across a wooden bridge; turn right here.

The only hill on the route comes after passing Citrus Avenue and turning right at a T-intersection; there's a 300-yard climb to a vantage point. Ride through a narrow tunnel under Ygnacio Valley Road, where the path continues next to a golf course and later a residential neighborhood. Watch out for blind corners, and ride carefully through the barriers at every intersection; they're barely wide enough for standard handlebars.

Finish the loop by passing John Muir Hospital and crossing busy Ygnacio Valley Road at a signal crosswalk. Ride the north sidewalk to Marchbanks Drive and complete the loop.

The canals are managed by East Bay Regional Park District (Contra Costa Canal) and the Walnut Creek Parks Department (Ygnacio Canal).

3.5 Tunnel under Ygnacio Valley Road.

4.4 Arbolado Drive.

4.6 Keep right along canal.

4.7 Oak Grove Road.

5.5 Walnut Avenue.

6.9 San Miguel Park on right.

7.0 John Muir Hospital.

7.2 Cross Ygnacio Valley Road at light and take sidewalk.

7.4 Left on Marchbanks Drive.

7.7 End ride at Heather Farms City Park.

■

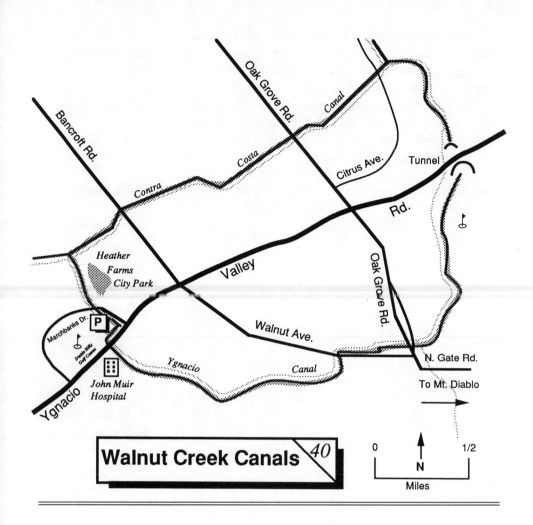

Walnut Creek Canals 40

0   1/2

N

Miles

Bibliography

Anderson, Charles. *Mountain Bike Trails of the Bay Area.* Palo Alto: Omega Printing, 1984.

Arrigoni, Patricia. *Making the Most of Marin, A California Guide.* Novato: Presidio Press, 1981.

Butler, Phyllis Filiberti. *The Valley of Santa Clara, Historic Buildings, 1792–1920.* San Jose: Junior League of San Jose, 1975.

Davis, Dorothy. *A Pictorial History of Pleasanton.* Pleasanton: Pleasanton National Bicentennial Committee, 1976.

Emmanuels, George. *California's Contra Costa County, An Illustrated History.* Fresno: Panorama West Books, 1986.

Futcher, Jane. *Marin: the Place, the People; Profile of a California County.* New York: Holt, Reinhart, Winston, 1981.

Graves, Al and Ted Wurm. *The Crookedest Railroad in the World.* Glendale: Trans-Anglo Books, 1983.

Halley, William. *The Centennial Year Book of Alameda County.* Oakland.

Hynding, Alan. *From Frontier to Suburb, The Story of San Mateo Peninsula.* Belmont: Star Publishing Company, 1982.

Kneiss, Gilbert H. *Redwood Railways.* San Diego: Howell-North Press, 1956.

Koch, Margaret. *Santa Cruz County, Parade of the Past.* Fresno: Valley Publishers, 1973.

Lewis, Oscar. *San Francisco: Mission to Metropolis.* San Diego: Howell-North Books, 1966.

MacGregor, Bruce and Truesdale, Richard. *A Centennial: South Pacific Coast.* Boulder: Pruett Publishing Company, 1982.

McCarthy, Frances Florence. *The History of Mission San Jose California 1779–1835.* Fresno: Academy Library Guild, 1958.

Neumann, Phyllis. *Sonoma County Bike Trails.* Penngrove: 1978.

O'Hare, Carol. *A Bicyclist's Guide to Bay Area History.* Sunnyvale: Bear Flag Books, 1985.

Payne, Stephen M. *Santa Clara County, Harvest of Change.* Northridge: Windsor Publications, 1987.

Richards, Gilbert. *Crossroads, People, and Events of the Redwoods of San Mateo County.* Woodside: Gilbert Richards Publications, 1973.

Sandoval, John. *The History of Washington Township.* Castro Valley: 1985.

Stanger, Frank M. *South from San Francisco.* San Mateo: San Mateo County Historical Association, 1963.

State of California, *Geologic Guidebook of the San Francisco Bay Counties.* San Francisco: Division of Mines, 1951.

Tays, George, ed. *Historical Landmarks & Sites of Alameda County California.* Oakland: Alameda County Library, 1938.

Town of Danville. *Danville, Portrait of 125 Years.* Alamo: Robert Pease & Co.

Verardo, Denzil and Verardo, Jennie Dennis. *Napa Valley, From Golden Fields to Purple Harvest.* Northridge: Windsor Publications, 1986.

Whitnam, Dorothy L. *An Outdoor Guide to the San Francisco Bay Area.* Berkeley: Wilderness Press, 1976.

Index

About the Author

Ray Hosler has been bicycling and writing in the Bay Area since 1977. He rides some 5000 miles a year, more than twice as many miles as he drives his car. This is his fifth book, on subjects ranging from foot care, to massage, to triathlon training. He is a former weekly bicycle columnist for the San Francisco *Chronicle*. He lives in Santa Clara, California.

For more information about bicycle organizations, bikes on Bay Area bridges, public bike lockers, and bicycles on public transit contact the **Regional Bicycle Advisory Committee,** 3313 Grand Ave., Oakland CA 94610. (415) 452-1221.